SECRETS TO WINNING A SCHOLARSHIP

Mark Kantrowitz

Publisher of Fastweb and FinAid

TABLE OF CONTENTS

FOREWORD

Look, I know you're in a bind. College has always been expensive, but if your family is like millions of others trying to cope with all the fallout from the financial crisis, it may be even more expensive than you (or your parents) anticipated. Maybe your parents can't help out as much as they'd like, now that they know they need to focus on saving more for retirement. Or maybe they were intending to tap your home's equity to cover a big chunk of the college bills, but that's looking less doable if you happen to live in an area hard hit by the bursting of the real estate bubble.

And it's not as if college costs have come down recently. Anything but, right?

So here's the deal: You need to make sure you do everything – and I mean *everything* – to keep the cost of college down. If you're going to be paying your way through school, that's a no-brainer. But even if your family will be covering some of the costs, you and I both know it would be a major help if you could help keep the bill as low as possible.

Secrets to Winning a Scholarship is your required reading for doing just that. Scholarships make college more affordable. Every dollar you win in a scholarship is a dollar you (or your family) do not have to pay out of your own pocket or it is a dollar less that needs to be borrowed. You're crazy to not put some serious time and effort into the process. And you couldn't have a better "teacher" to show you the way. Mark has an encyclopedic knowledge of college financing that I have valued for years. In this book, he delivers clear advice on exactly what you need to do (and not do!) to increase your odds of landing a scholarship — from how to find scholarships that can be a good match, to how to nail the interview with the scholarship committee. Mark's ready to help you lower your college costs. What are you waiting for?

— *Suze Orman*

INTRODUCTION

This book provides practical, clear and concise advice about how to find and win scholarships and fellowships. It is direct and to the point, providing a high concentration of useful information.

Scholarships are free money for your college education. More than 1.5 million scholarships worth more than $3.5 billion are awarded by donors, philanthropists, foundations, corporations and other charitable organizations every year. Most scholarships are based on special qualifications, such as academic, artistic or athletic talent. Some are based on special circumstances (e.g., one of your parents is a cancer survivor) or even where you live (e.g., community-based scholarships). Some are based on demonstrated financial need. While there is a lot of competition for scholarships, they can play an important role in your plan for paying for college.

Unlike student loans, scholarships provide money for college that does not need to be repaid. Every dollar you win in scholarships is potentially a dollar less you have to borrow.

Rather than providing a long list of scholarships, this book assumes that you will use the free Fastweb scholarship-matching service at www.fastweb.com to search for scholarships that match your background profile. After all, the typical inch-thick printed listing of scholarships is as much as a year old by the time it is published, while the Fastweb database is updated daily and notifies you automatically when a new scholarship that matches your profile is added to the database. Instead, this book concentrates on providing insider tips and insights on how to maximize your chances of winning a scholarship.

(This book does, however, include a few top-ten lists of the most prestigious and most lucrative scholarships in an appendix.)

If you're looking for lists of the most prestigious, lucrative or unusual scholarships; scholarships for average students; or academic scholarships, visit www.finaid.org/scholarships.

International students who are interested in studying in the United States of America should visit www.edupass.org.

Students from the United States of America who are interested in studying abroad should visit www.finaid.org/studyabroad.

ABOUT THE AUTHOR

Mark Kantrowitz is a nationally recognized expert on student financial aid and paying for college. He is the founder and publisher of FinAid.org, the leading source for clear and objective student financial-aid information, advice and tools. He is also the publisher of Fastweb.com, the most popular and most comprehensive free scholarship-matching web site. Together, these sites have helped more than 50 million students and parents figure out how to pay for college. Mark is also the author of the best-selling book *FastWeb College Gold: The Step-by-Step Guide to Paying for College* (Collins, September 2006).

As a recognized financial-aid expert for more than two decades, Mark has been called to testify before Congress about financial aid on several occasions and is interviewed regularly by news outlets, including the *Wall Street Journal*, the *New York Times*, the *Washington Post*, the *Los Angeles Times*, the *Boston Globe*, the *San Francisco Chronicle*, the *Chicago Tribune*, the *Baltimore Sun*, the *Dallas Morning News*, MSN, CNN, NBC, ABC, CBS, NPR, CNBC, *USA Today*, the Associated Press, Reuters, Bloomberg, *Money* magazine, *SmartMoney*, *Forbes*, *Fortune*, *BusinessWeek*, *Kiplinger's*, *U.S. News & World Report*, *Newsweek*, *MarketWatch*, *University Business*, *Inside Higher Ed* and the *Chronicle of Higher Education*. He is the curator of the Student Loans topic page on the *New York Times* web site, a member of the editorial board of the Council on Law in Higher Education, a member of the editorial advisory board of Bottom Line/Personal and a member of the board of directors of the National Scholarship Providers Association. He writes a weekly column for MainStreet.com and the weekly *Ask Kantro* column for Fastweb.

Mark's work in financial aid has been recognized by many awards, including a Meritorious Achievement Award from the National Association of Student Financial Aid Administrators, a Special Award from the College Board, the President's Award from the National Association of Graduate and Professional Students and the Jefferson Medal from the American Institute for Public Service. He was also the Pennsylvania state finalist for the Congressional Medal of Honor Society's Above & Beyond Citizen Honors.

Mark is ABD on a Ph.D. in computer science from Carnegie Mellon University (CMU), has a Master of Science degree in computer science from CMU and Bachelor of Science degrees in mathematics and philosophy from the Massachusetts Institute of Technology (MIT) and is an alumnus of the Research Science Institute program established by Admiral H.G. Rickover. He is a member of the board of trustees of the Center for Excellence in Education.

Not surprisingly, he was able to pay for his undergraduate education through scholarships and summer employment and his graduate education entirely through fellowships and grants. Some of the major scholarships, fellowships and education awards Mark has been awarded include the National Science Foundation Graduate Fellowship, the Hertz Foundation Research Fellowship Grant, the MIT Karl Taylor Compton Prize, the MIT William L. Stewart Jr. Award, the Courant Institute Prize for Mathematical Talent, the Westinghouse Science Talent Search, the Massachusetts State Science Fair First Award (four-time winner), the USA Mathematical Olympiad, the Massachusetts State Math Olympiad, the New England Math League and the Continental Math League. Mark is a member of the Phi Kappa Phi and Sigma Xi honor societies, and a national member of the Alpha Epsilon Lambda honor society of graduate and professional students.

Mark is a cancer survivor, is the author of five books and holds seven patents, with several additional patents pending.

ACKNOWLEDGEMENTS

Thank you to the following people for reviewing and commenting on drafts of this book:

- Carlos Adrian, Gates Millennium Scholars Program

- Kevin Byrne, Director, U.S. Education, Michael & Susan Dell Foundation

- Roger Lehecka, The Lenfest Foundation

- David Levy, Director of Financial Aid, Scripps College

- Cathy Makunga, Sr. Director for Scholarship Programs, Hispanic Scholarship Fund

- Colleen J. Quint, Executive Director, Sen. George J. Mitchell Scholarship Research Institute

- Patti A. Ross, Vice President, Coca-Cola Scholars Foundation, Inc.

- Timothy G. Snow, President, George Snow Scholarship Fund

- Joe Wilcox, Scholarship Coordinator, University of Texas at Austin

Thank you also to the Fastweb staff, including Andrea Abegglen, Jill Bodino, Mark Nelson, Charles Purdy, Jacy Shillan, Janet Swaysland, Allison Wagner and Lauren Anderson Youngblood, for their help and suggestions.

WHO WINS SCHOLARSHIPS?

There are many myths about who wins scholarships. This chapter debunks a few of these myths. However, don't let the following dose of reality stop you from trying to win scholarships. Scholarships are an important part of your plan for paying for college.

Your chances of winning a scholarship depend on your efforts, your academic and extracurricular background and how well you prepare your applications. This book will help you strategically position yourself to win as many scholarships as possible. But your chances for success will ultimately depend on you.

Very Few Students Win a Completely Free Ride

Very few students receive enough need-based and non-need-based grants to cover all college costs. Of students enrolled full-time at four-year colleges in 2007–08, only 0.3% received enough grants (including federal and state grants, institutional grants and private scholarships) to cover the full cost of attendance. Only 1.0% received enough grants to cover 90% or more of the cost of attendance; 3.4%, to cover 75% or more of the cost of attendance; and 14.3%, to cover more than half the cost of attendance.[1]

Roughly 0.2% of students enrolled full-time at four-year colleges used private scholarships totaling more than $15,000, 0.7% used

---

[1]   Many of the statistics mentioned in this book were calculated using the data analysis system for the 2007–08 National Postsecondary Student Aid Study (NPSAS). The NPSAS is a large survey conducted every four years by the National Center for Education Statistics at the U.S. Department of Education. The 2007–08 NPSAS surveyed 114,000 undergraduate students and 14,000 graduate and professional students. Other statistics are based on analyses of various Fastweb databases.

scholarships totaling more than $10,000, 1.8% used scholarships totaling more than $5,000 and 4.1% used scholarships totaling more than $2,500. Of the students winning scholarships, more than two-thirds (69.1%) used less than $2,500, representing roughly 9.2% of students enrolled full-time at four-year colleges.

This means that fewer than 20,000 students a year receive a completely free ride when one counts all types of grants, not just private scholarships. There are fewer than 250 private scholarships that provide enough money on their own to cover all college costs. Most full-tuition scholarships are awarded by less-popular colleges to attract talented students and meet enrollment goals.

But don't get discouraged. Winning scholarships is still an important part of your plan for paying for college. Every dollar you win in scholarships is a dollar less you have to borrow. Winning scholarships enables you to choose the college that is the best match for you, even if it happens to cost more than a less prestigious institution. And perhaps you'll be one of the few students each year who wins a gazillion dollars for college.

Students at Four-Year Colleges Win More Scholarships

You are more likely to win a private scholarship if you will be enrolled full-time at a four-year college or university. Students who are enrolled part-time or at a two-year institution are much less likely to win scholarships.

For example, according to the National Postsecondary Student Aid Study (NPSAS), 10.1% of students who were enrolled full-time in 2007–08 received a scholarship, compared with only 2.3% of students who were enrolled part-time. Similarly, 8.3% of students enrolled at four-year colleges won scholarships, compared with 2.6% of students enrolled at two-year colleges. More than three-quarters of scholarship recipients (77%) were enrolled at four-year colleges.

Among students who apply for financial aid and are enrolled full-time, those enrolled at four-year institutions are much more likely to win:

- 13.3% of full-time students at four-year institutions who applied for financial aid won scholarships worth $2,794 on average, compared with 4.5% of part-time students (average $2,579).

- 6.9% of full-time students at two-year institutions who applied for financial aid won scholarships worth $1,494 on average, compared with 3.3% of part-time students (average $1,459).

Four-year colleges represent almost a quarter (23.5%) of the student population but more than half (56.9%) of scholarship recipients and almost three-quarters (71.2%) of scholarship dollars.

Some Majors Are More Lucrative Than Others

The following table demonstrates that STEM fields (Science, Technology, Engineering and Mathematics) are more likely to win scholarships than non-STEM fields. Among applicants enrolled full-time/full-year at four-year colleges, 17.0% of students majoring in STEM fields win scholarships, compared with 12.1% of students majoring in non-STEM fields.

While most majors are intellectually valuable fields of study, the STEM fields add practical utility. Companies are more willing to offer scholarships in STEM fields, especially graduate-school fellowships, because STEM research produces solutions to important problems.

Major	Percentage Winning	Average Award
Math/Statistics	23.2%	$4,059
Engineering	17.6%	$3,075
Physical Sciences	17.1%	$3,180
Life Sciences	16.9%	$2,649
Education	15.0%	$2,420
Health	14.8%	$2,880
Social Sciences	12.7%	$3,063
Humanities	12.5%	$2,623
Computer Science	11.1%	$2,974
Business	9.1%	$2,828

Students with Good Grades Win More Scholarships

The following table demonstrates that having a higher grade point average (GPA) increases the odds of winning a scholarship for applicants who are enrolled full-time/full-year at a four-year college or university. The trend is similar for high school GPA and college GPA, but slightly better for a higher college GPA.

Cumulative Grade Point Average on a 4.0 Scale	High School GPA (% Winning Scholarships)	College GPA (% Winning Scholarships)
0.0-1.9 (D- to C)	5.7%	7.0%
2.0-2.4 (C to B-)	7.1%	9.1%
2.5-2.9 (B- to B)	9.5%	10.7%
3.0-3.4 (B to A-)	10.7%	13.1%

In comparison, the odds of winning an athletic scholarship are only 2.2% among students enrolled full-time at four-year colleges. (Among all students, not just those enrolled full-time at four-year colleges, the odds of winning an athletic scholarship are just 0.7%.)

While getting an A can increase your chances of winning a scholarship, it is important that you take challenging classes. Scholarship sponsors will look at your high school academic transcripts to see whether you got your good grades by taking only easy classes. They will also consider whether you took any Advanced Placement or honors classes. Of students who earned Advanced Placement credit in high school, 9.7% won scholarships, compared with 5.5% of students who did not. It is better to earn a solid B in a difficult class than to earn an A in an easy class.

Note that college-controlled scholarships based on academic merit are usually awarded by the college or university admissions office, the academic department or the office of the president, not the financial-aid office, which is focused primarily on financial aid based on financial need. Eligibility for these academic scholarships usually depends on having high standardized test scores and class rank. The scholarships are used as recruiting tools by less-competitive institutions. A list of full-tuition academic scholarships can be found at www.finaid.org/academicscholarships.

Of course, there are many scholarships that don't depend on your having a good GPA. Some of the more well-known examples include:

- The David Letterman Telecommunications Scholarship at Ball State University for average students who nevertheless have a creative mind.

- Duck Brand Duck Tape Stuck at Prom Contest for creating a prom costume out of duct tape.

- The AXA Achievement Scholarship for outstanding achievement in non-academic activities.

For more information about these and similar scholarships, visit www.finaid.org/average. Also search the Fastweb scholarship database at www.fastweb.com, which will automatically show you only the scholarships that match your background. If you don't have good grades, your scholarship matches will include only awards that do not require that you have good grades.

Students with Good Test Scores Win More Scholarships

The following tables demonstrate that having a higher combined SAT score or ACT score increases the odds of winning a scholarship. It shows the relationship between the combined SAT score (the sum of SAT I verbal and math scores) or ACT composite score and the likelihood of winning scholarships. Both tables include data from students who took either the SAT or ACT tests, with ACT scores converted to the equivalent SAT score range and vice versa.

SAT Combined Score	Probability of Winning a Scholarship
< 700	2.6%
700 to 800	4.2%
800 to 900	5.4%
900 to 1000	5.8%
1000 to 1100	7.4%
1100 to 1200	8.5%
1200 to 1300	11.2%
1300 to 1400	13.2%

Students with combined SAT scores of 1000 or more are more than twice as likely to win a scholarship as students with combined SAT scores under 1000. The odds of winning a scholarship are 9.2% for students with combined SAT scores of 1000 or more, compared with 3.8% for students with combined SAT scores of less than 1000. (The average combined SAT score is about 1000.)

While getting a good score on the SAT or ACT can improve your odds of winning a scholarship, only about 3.5% of all scholarships have an SAT or ACT score requirement.

ACT Composite Score	Probability of Winning a Scholarship
< 15	2.6%
15-17	4.7%
18-20	5.6%
21-23	7.3%
24-26	8.3%
27-29	11.1%
30-36	14.2%

Students with an ACT composite score of 21 or more are more than twice as likely to win a scholarship as students with an ACT composite score under 21. The odds of winning a scholarship are 9.0% for students with an ACT composite score of 21 or more, compared with 3.7% for students with an ACT composite score under 21. (The average ACT composite score is about 21.)

Students Enrolled at More Selective and Expensive Colleges Are More Likely to Win Scholarships

The following table shows that students who are enrolled at more-selective four-year public and non-profit colleges are more likely to win scholarships.

This trend is partly due to selection bias, where the more talented students are more likely to enroll at the more selective colleges. But it is also partly due to private scholarships enabling choice, since the scholarships allow lower-income students to enroll at more prestigious colleges despite the higher cost. For example, 4.2% of students enrolled at colleges with a cost of attendance under $20,000 win scholarships, compared with 10.7% of students enrolled at colleges that cost $20,000 or more. Of students enrolled at non-profit colleges, 10.2% win scholarships, compared with 5.1% of students at public colleges and 1.5% of students at for-profit colleges.

College Selectivity	Probability of Winning a Scholarship		
	All Students	1st Year Students	2nd – 4th Year Students
Open Admission	6.2%	5.9%	6.6%
Minimally Selective	8.3%	11.2%	7.2%
Moderately Selective	9.3%	14.1%	8.0%
Very Selective	10.2%	16.8%	8.7%

The Third-Generation Effect

Students who are third-generation immigrants are more likely to win scholarships than students who are first- or second-generation immigrants.

First-generation immigrants are U.S. citizens who were not born in the U.S. and whose parents were not born in the U.S. Second-generation immigrants are U.S. citizens who were born in the U.S. but with at least one foreign-born parent. Third-generation immigrants are U.S. citizens who were born to U.S. citizen parents who were born in the U.S.

Only 3.8% of first-generation immigrants win college scholarships, compared with 4.4% of second-generation immigrants and 6.0% of third-generation immigrants.

The third-generation effect persists even when limited to students who are pursuing Bachelor's degrees. For example, 7.2% of first-generation immigrants and 7.3% of second-generation immigrants win scholarships, compared with 9.3% of third generation immigrants.

The Race Myth

Contrary to a common misconception, minority students are less likely to win scholarships than white students among applicants enrolled full-time/full-year at four-year colleges and universities. The main exception is Native-American students, who represent a very small percentage of recipients. (The statistics for Native-American students may lack statistical significance due to the small sample size.) Minority students represent 33.8% of applicants but only 28.5% of recipients.

Race	Percent of Recipients	Percent Winning	Average Award
White	71.5%	14.4%	$2,645
Black or African American	10.5%	11.4%	$2,962
Hispanic or Latino	8.1%	9.1%	$2,353
Asian	4.4%	10.5%	$3,170
American Indian or Alaska Native	1.4%	32.7%	$3,967
More Than One Race	3.4%	16.0%	$4,891
All Minority Students	28.5%	11.2%	$3,167

You Don't Have to Be Poor to Win Scholarships

There's a myth that only students who are poor win scholarships. Middle-income students are more likely to win scholarships than lower- or upper-income students. Among students enrolled full-time at a four-year college, 10.6% of students with a family adjusted gross income (AGI) of less than $50,000 won scholarships in 2007–08, compared with 13.8% of students with a family AGI of $50,000 to $100,000 and 10.8% of students with a family AGI of more than $100,000. In addition, lower-income students are more likely to enroll part-time and at two-year colleges and so are less likely to win scholarships.

If the statistics are adjusted according to the number of students applying for any type of financial aid, 11.3% of students with family

AGI of less than $50,000 won scholarships in 2007-08, compared with 15.6% of students with a family AGI of $50,000 to $100,000 and 14.3% of students with a family AGI of more than $100,000. Low-income students outnumber middle- and upper-income students and are more likely to apply for aid, so the lower percentages for low-income students are not due to self-selection.

Students from Private High Schools Win More Scholarships

Students who graduate from private high schools win slightly more scholarships and other forms of merit-based student aid than students from public high schools, but not enough to compensate for the higher cost of private-school tuition. Moreover, these students are more likely to enroll at higher-cost colleges, leading to a higher out-of-pocket cost. A private high school education does not lead to a free ticket to college.

Type of High School	Private Scholarships		Institutional Grants		Total Merit-Based Grants	
	%	Average	%	Average	%	Average
Public	12.3%	$2,631	23.9%	$6,293	27.0%	$5,700
Private	10.0%	$3,463	28.5%	$7,327	30.9%	$6,705

This demonstrates that students who graduated from private high schools tend to get about $1,000 more in merit-based aid per year than students who graduated from public high schools. But the cost of private-school tuition exceeds the financial benefit of winning more merit-based aid.

Moreover, the higher amount of merit-based aid may have more to do with the distribution of students across public, non-profit and for-profit colleges. As the following table demonstrates, students who attended public high schools are more likely to attend public colleges, while students who attended private high schools are more likely to attend private non-profit colleges. The average college cost of attendance is higher as a result for students who attended private high schools ($28,435 versus $24,062), perhaps explaining the larger aid packages. This ultimately causes the out-of-pocket cost (cost of attendance minus grant aid) to be higher for the students who attended private high schools despite the higher merit-based grants ($22,289 vs. $18,704).

Distribution of Students by College Type			
Type of High School	Public Colleges	Non-Profit Colleges	For-Profit Colleges
Public	65.5%	26.7%	7.9%
Private	47.3%	48.5%	4.2%

Community Service and Volunteering Matter

Scholarship providers are public-spirited, giving back to the community. They like to see similar qualities in the students they support, even if the scholarships are not awarded to recognize community service and volunteering. Many scholarship programs include a community-service component, requiring that scholarship recipients engage in a volunteer activity.

You can increase your chances of winning a scholarship by participating in volunteer activities. Depth and length of commitment are more important than breadth, so pick a single volunteer activity and devote a lot of time to it instead of changing your volunteer activity each year. Pick a problem and try to develop innovative ways of solving it. The challenge of solving real world problems can be very satisfying, especially since you will be making a difference.

Scholarship providers try to pick scholars who best match their goals, and this usually includes a goal of enhancing the reputation and prestige of the organization. Scholars who are committed to helping others are more likely to win than a student who is self-centered.

You can also earn money for college by volunteering through the AmeriCorps program. For example, the Segal AmeriCorps Education Award (www.americorps.gov) provides several thousand dollars for each year of full-time volunteer service, prorated for part-time efforts. The maximum education award is pegged to the maximum Federal Pell Grant. It's a great way of doing well by doing good.

Another great resource is DoSomething.org, which helps young people make a difference in their communities. They are the largest organization in the US for teenagers and social change. Besides providing grants and other resources, they also sponsor one of the top ten scholarships for community service.

Other scholarships for community service can be found on the FinAid site at www.finaid.org/volunteering and through the free Fastweb scholarship matching service at www.fastweb.com.

BASIC STRATEGIES FOR WINNING SCHOLARSHIPS

The best strategy for winning scholarships is to apply for as many scholarships as possible. Here's why:

It's a Numbers Game

Most scholarship sponsors have more qualified applications than available funds, so even qualified applicants get rejected. Get used to rejection, as each win will be accompanied by a lot of losses.

To improve your chances of winning a scholarship, apply for as many scholarships as possible. Scholarship competitions are not lotteries, since a student who is better qualified and a stronger match to the sponsor's goals is more likely to win the scholarship. But you are competing against many other perhaps equally qualified candidates for a limited pool of money. So even if you are one of the most talented applicants, there is still a bit of luck involved in whether your application stands out enough to be selected as a winner. Winning a scholarship is based on both skill and luck. Who wins the scholarship may depend on arbitrary or even random factors. Therefore, applying to more scholarship programs gives you more opportunities to win a scholarship.

But apply only to scholarships for which you are qualified. You may be a wonderful and talented person, but the scholarship sponsor won't look at your application if you don't satisfy the prerequisites. They have enough qualified applicants that near-misses will not be considered.

You can't win if you don't apply. Don't be among the nearly one in four students who never applies for financial aid.

The Psychology of Winning

Students who win scholarships are highly motivated to succeed. Failure is an obstacle to be circumvented, not a stumbling block. You won't win every time and will probably lose more often than you win. Even very talented students have to apply to at least a dozen scholarships to win just one or two. Persistence and stamina are keys to success in winning scholarships. Keep playing the game despite the failures. Losses are just an opportunity to learn from your mistakes.

Remember, applying for scholarships is a numbers game, so there may be a lot of rejections before you win an award. There will be many times when you will be mystified as to why the scholarship selection committee didn't choose your application to win the scholarship. For example, when I was a high school senior I entered the Thomas Edison/Max McGraw Scholarship Program with a project entitled "The Electronic Clipboard" that described an approach to implementing a touch-sensitive LCD display with such applications as an electronic clipboard (with handwriting recognition), an artist's sketchpad and a keyboard-less computer. My proposal was selected as a semi-finalist but did not win a scholarship. Perhaps it was a bit too far ahead of its time, predating the Apple Newton by five years, the Palm Pilot by twelve years and the iPod Touch by more than two decades.[2]

---

2   I nevertheless maintained a long-term interest in the development of this type of technology. When I was a research scientist at Just Research in the late 1990s, I developed a dictionary-less spelling-correction algorithm for the Palm Pilot that reduced the Graffiti handwriting-recognition error rate by 30%.

SEARCHING FOR SCHOLARSHIPS

Before you can apply for scholarships, you have to find them. This chapter discusses tools and strategies for searching for scholarships.

Start Searching As Soon As Possible

The sooner you start searching for scholarships, the more scholarships you will find and the greater your chances of winning a scholarship. Some deadlines are as early as August or September. If you wait until January to search for scholarships, you will miss deadlines for half the awards. Searching for scholarships is a year-round activity, not just one for the spring of your senior year in high school.

Scholarships are also not limited to high school seniors. There are many scholarships for grades 9, 10 and 11, as well as scholarships for current college students. The Fastweb site, www.fastweb.com, will match you with all of these scholarships. There are even scholarships available to children in grades K-8, such as awards for community service, art and essay competitions, geography and spelling bees, contests for the best peanut butter and jelly sandwich, math competitions and prizes for the best mibster (a marbles champion).

The FinAid site, www.finaid.org, is a free web site with comprehensive financial-aid information, advice and tools. It includes a list of scholarships for students under age 13 at www.finaid.org/age13, in addition to specialized lists of scholarships, such as unusual scholarships, prestigious scholarships, community service scholarships and scholarships for cancer survivors.[3]

---

3   The Children's Online Privacy Protection Act (COPPA) prohibits web sites from collecting information from children under age 13 without verifiable parental consent. Accordingly, none of the free scholarship-matching web sites will allow young children to register. This list appears on the FinAid site because FinAid does not have a registration process.

Don't wait until you've been admitted to college to start thinking about how you will pay for it. Unfortunately, many families wait until after they've applied for admission to start searching for scholarships, meaning that they miss many opportunities. The sooner you start searching, the more scholarships you will find. This increases your chances of winning a scholarship.

Scholarships with earlier deadlines may be a little less competitive because fewer students submit applications. On the other hand, these students tend to be better organized, so the competition may be a little tougher. Several of the most prestigious and generous scholarships have deadlines in the fall.

Continue searching for scholarships even after you enroll in college. There are many scholarships that are open only to current college students. (The Fastweb scholarship-matching service, www.fastweb.com, will automatically email you information about new awards that match your background and will continue to do so when you are in college. However, it is a good idea to review and update your personal profile at least once a year to ensure that you match as many awards as possible. Add any new awards, activities and accomplishments to your personal profile.)

Some scholarships require advance preparation, so it is important to allow enough time to complete the application. For example, you will need to spend at least a month or two preparing a math or science project for the state science fair or creating a prom costume out of duct tape.

How to Search for Scholarships

The best way to search for scholarships is to use a free scholarship-matching service like Fastweb.com. It's easy! It takes only about 30 to 60 minutes to complete a personal profile highlighting your background, such as your grades, test scores, interests, hobbies and activities. Fastweb then matches your profile against a very large database of scholarships and you receive an immediate list of all the scholarships that match your profile. This targeted matching process helps you focus on just the scholarships for which you are eligible. The typical high school senior will match about 100 scholarships, depending on the completeness of the profile. Then it's up to you to apply for the scholarships and, hopefully, win.

The Fastweb database is updated daily, so it is always up-to-date, unlike books which usually have information that is at least several months old on the date the book is published. An added benefit is that Fastweb will automatically send you an email message whenever a new scholarship that matches your background is added to the database. The Fastweb site also provides you with timely news, information and advice. All of these services are completely free.

It is probably a good idea to search one of the other free scholarship databases in addition to Fastweb. That will give you added confidence than you've found all the scholarships for which you are eligible. A list of other free scholarship web sites can be found on the FinAid site at www.finaid.org/scholarships. Never pay to search a scholarship database, as the fee-based scholarship search services are not as accurate, comprehensive or up-to-date as the free online services.

Don't compare scholarship databases based on the advertised number of scholarships, as each database uses a different method to estimate the number of awards and these methods are usually inaccurate. Very few sponsors provide data on the number of scholarships and the total dollars awarded. Since these figures do not form a statistical normal distribution, multiplying the average number of scholarships per scholarship program or the average award amount by the total number of scholarship programs usually results in a gross overestimate of the size of the database. There are several very large scholarship programs that will skew the averages if they are included in the sample used to calculate the averages. Some databases will also inflate their figures by counting federal and state aid as part of the total, even though they are not private scholarships.

You can also find information about scholarships in scholarship-listing books in your local public library or bookstore. While scholarship-listing books do not provide targeted matching, they are still useful for random exploration. This can help you find awards in new fields and broaden your interests. Generally, scholarship books will be found in the reference section of the public library or bookstore, near books about jobs and careers. Before you rely on any scholarship listing book, check the publication date. Scholarship listing books that are more than a year or two old are too dated to be useful because approximately 1 in 10 scholarship programs change each year.

Look for Local Scholarships

Look for information about local awards posted on bulletin boards near the guidance counselor's office or local college's financial-aid office or the jobs and careers section of the local public library. Some guidance counselors publicize scholarships in the school bulletin or on their high school's web site. Others distribute scholarship booklets to their students. Also look in your local newspaper, especially in the coupon section. Many national brands — such as Tylenol, Coca Cola, Discover Card and Jif Peanut Butter — offer scholarships that they promote in the coupon section of the Sunday newspaper. Fastweb includes most local awards, but some local awards do not want to be included in any of the national scholarship databases.

Be thorough in searching for local scholarships. Besides the free online scholarship matching services like Fastweb, ask every organization with which you are associated whether they offer any scholarships. These include your employer, your parent's employer, unions and fraternal organizations, religious organizations, ethnic groups, cultural organizations, volunteer groups, clubs, your local PTA and your high school. Ask local businesses, such as community banks, grocery stores, bowling alleys and any other business that is not part of a national chain, whether they sponsor scholarships for local students. (The national chains also sponsor scholarships either nationally or within their local communities, but these scholarships are usually well publicized and can be found in scholarship databases like Fastweb.) The city chamber of commerce might have information about local businesses that award scholarships. Also ask your high school guidance counselor and the financial-aid administrators at nearby colleges about small local awards from community-based organizations such as your local PTA, rotary club and community foundations.

Googling for Grants

All of the major free scholarship matching web sites routinely use Google, Yahoo, Lycos, AltaVista and other search engines to search for new scholarships to add to their databases. Some even have their own custom web spiders. So looking for scholarships using a search engine is unlikely to help you find new awards that aren't already included in one of the online scholarship search tools. However, if you are looking for scholarships in a specialized field of study, Google and other search engines can sometimes uncover a few good leads.

To search for scholarships using a web search engine, add the word "scholarship" or "scholarships" or similar keywords to the search query along with the name of the organization or activity. (Some search engines, like Google, treat plural and singular word forms separately, so you should try the search with each variant.) FinAid has a tool that makes this easier at www.finaid.org/websearch.

Good keywords to use include "scholarships," "fellowships," "foundation," "association," "endowment," "award," "scholar," "contest," "competition," "grant," "trust" and "application deadline." Also use geographic locations like the name of your hometown. If a name is more than just one word, enclosing it in quotation marks can help narrow the matches. For example, try searching for "average scholarships" with and without the quotes.

Sometimes, adding the word "scholarships" to a query more than once can change the search results. This added emphasis gives more weight to pages that mention the word "scholarships" more frequently.

Try to use search terms that are both more and less specific than the subject of the search, as well as synonyms and parallel terminology. For example, if you are searching for scholarships for leukemia survivors, also search for "cancer scholarships" and "lymphoma scholarships." Some of the scholarships for cancer survivors will match even if they don't specifically mention leukemia.

Answer Optional Questions to Maximize Your Matches

Even though it takes a little longer and can be a bit tedious, try to answer all of the optional questions. Students who complete the background profile more thoroughly match twice as many awards as students who respond to only the required questions.

To answer the optional questions on the Fastweb site, click on the "My Profile" link in the upper right hand corner of the page after logging in. Click on the "edit" links to the right of each section of the personal profile, especially the Student Activities and Parent Activities sections. Several scrolling menus will appear, each with a long list of possible choices. Review the choices carefully. Many awards will appear in your list of matches only if you check off the corresponding profile choice. For example, you must check the boxes for "newspaper editor," "yearbook staff," "cancer survivor" or "single parent" to have the relevant scholarships included in your scholarship search results.

The following chart shows the impact of the completeness of the profile on the number of matches, based on Fastweb data. (About a third of the questions on the Fastweb personal profile are required.)

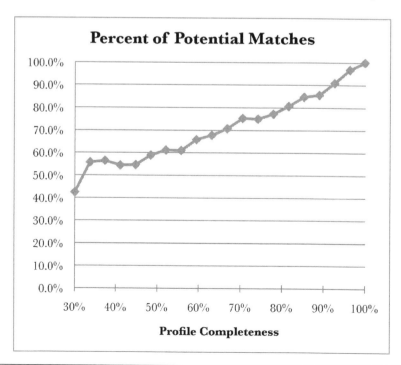

The following chart illustrates the distribution of students on the Fastweb site according to profile completeness.

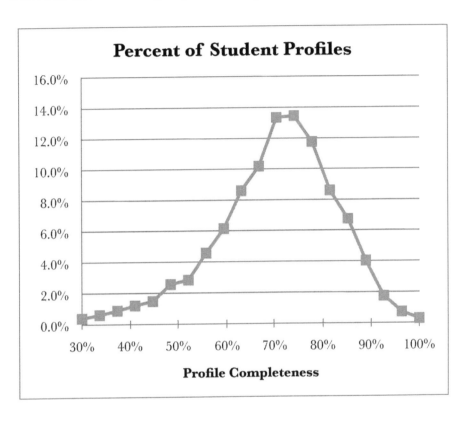

Look for Near-Miss Matches

Slight changes in some of your qualifications can have a significant impact on the number of scholarships for which you are eligible. For example, improving your GPA by 0.1 points or your SAT score by 50 to 100 points can help you match more scholarships.

Near-miss matches can motivate you to improve your academic performance. But apply for an award only if you qualify. You have to improve your grades before you can apply.

Several questions in the scholarship search profile include long lists of possible choices, such as hobbies and activities. Read through the lists carefully to make sure you haven't overlooked anything. Otherwise, you might miss awards that are more general, such as scholarships for skateboarding, bowling, surfing, beef ambassador, vegetarians or community service. Most questions in the profile are included because each possible answer triggers the inclusion of one or more scholarships. Even your last name can potentially match a scholarship.

Pursue Less Competitive Scholarships

For students who are pursuing a Bachelor's degree on a full-time basis, the raw odds of winning a scholarship are about 1 in 8. Some of the more prestigious and lucrative scholarship programs are much more competitive, with odds of about 1 in 250 to 1 in 500. But there are also many less competitive scholarships available. It is easier to win these scholarships because there are fewer students competing for them. These scholarships are included in the Fastweb scholarship database along with the more competitive awards.

Some scholarships are less competitive because fewer students qualify for them. These include scholarships with narrow eligibility criteria, such as scholarships with geographic restrictions or that require membership in a particular organization. Examples include awards that are restricted to local residents, such as scholarships sponsored by community foundations or awarded to students who attended a specific high school. Examples of awards that require membership in a particular organization include scholarships restricted to the membership of a local religious institution, ethnic group or cultural organization and scholarships that require membership in a professional association, fraternity or sorority, or any other type of organization. College-controlled merit-based awards also tend to be less competitive.

Some scholarships are less competitive because the requirements are more obscure and specialized. For example, fewer students participate in equestrian sports (including rodeo), water polo and archery. Scholarships for certain majors may also be less competitive, such as agriculture and farming, natural resources, first responders (EMS, police, fire and ambulance), surveying and photogrammetry, national security and risk management, insurance and actuarial science programs. Scholarships that may be used only for a restricted purpose (e.g., study abroad in a more remote country) are also less competitive. This is why it is important to complete scholarship search profiles thoroughly, as you must list involvement in archery in order to match archery awards.

Some scholarships are less competitive because fewer qualified students apply for them. Many students will refuse to apply for small scholarships because they don't cover all the college costs. It seems strange to turn down free money, but scholarships that do not specify an award amount or where the award amount is less than $1,000 are much less competitive than scholarships that offer thousands of dollars to the winner. Students also seem to dismiss essay, art and poetry competitions.

Some scholarships are less competitive because the sponsors do not publicize the opportunities well. For example, some small local awards deliberately avoid being listed in any of the national scholarship databases because they do not want to be inundated with too many qualified applicants.

Don't Skip Small Scholarships

It is worth repeating: Don't skip small scholarships.

Apply for every scholarship for which you are eligible, no matter how small (or how large). Every dollar you win in scholarships is a dollar less you have to borrow.

Your chances of winning a small scholarship are greater than your chances of winning a more lucrative scholarship because they are less competitive. But winning several small scholarships can add up to big money.

Entering small scholarship competitions can be a good way of practicing for the bigger awards. Essays can often be reused on multiple scholarship applications with slight tweaks, saving you a lot of time. With each application, you can refine your pitch, improving your chances of winning a scholarship. Winning small scholarships also adds credentials that can help you win a bigger scholarship. Every time you win a scholarship, you add a line to your resume. Winning a scholarship is a mark of excellence, indicating that someone thought it worthwhile to invest his or her money in your future.

A $500 scholarship may seem small compared with annual college costs of $25,000 or more a year — just 2% of the totalbut that's $500 you won't have to borrow to pay for college. Moreover, a $500 reduction in education debt will ultimately save you $1,000, since every dollar you spend using student-loan money will cost you as much as two dollars by the time you've paid off the debt.[4]

Also, consider that if you have a 1 in 10 chance of winning a $500 scholarship and it takes you about an hour to complete the application, that's the equivalent of earning $50 an hour.[5] Very few high school students can find a more financially rewarding use of their time.

---

4   Assuming a 20-year term, the total payments on a student loan are about 1.8 to 2.1 times the original amount borrowed for federal education loans and as much as 3.7 for private student loans, based on typical interest rates.

5    $500/winner x 1 winner/10 applicants is the equivalent of $50/applicant. The next page explains the related concept of *expected value* in greater detail.

TIPS ON WINNING SCHOLARSHIPS

Now that you've identified several scholarships and are ready to apply for them, here are a few tips on how to increase your chances of winning the awards.

Prioritize Your Applications

Ideally, you should apply to every scholarship for which you are qualified. But if you have a limited amount of time available to apply for scholarships, prioritize your applications by both the deadlines and the expected value of the scholarship.

The *expected value* of a scholarship is the product of the award amount multiplied by the probability of winning the scholarship. Prioritizing by the expected value will maximize the total amount of money you are likely to win. For example, consider two scholarships, one of which is more lucrative (and hence more competitive) and the other of which is much smaller but also offers much better odds of winning. The more lucrative scholarship offers \$25,000 but only 1 in 400 applicants win the award, so the expected value is \$25,000 x 1/400 = \$62.50. The smaller scholarship offers only \$1,000 but your odds of winning it are 1 in 10, so the expected value is \$1,000 x 1/10 = \$100.00. Clearly, you are better off pursuing the smaller scholarship because of the better expected value. Note that if the odds of winning the more lucrative scholarship were 1 in 100 instead of 1 in 400, the expected value would increase to \$250.00.

Of course, such a quantitative approach to prioritizing applications should be informed by more qualitative factors, such as the degree to which one scholarship is a better fit to your background, increasing your chances of winning it beyond the raw odds. If you are a perfect match for the scholarship's selection criteria, you might want to apply even if you're competing against more than 100,000 other students.

Use a Calendar and Checklist to Get Organized

If you miss an application deadline, you will lose any chance of winning the award. Scholarship programs do not accept late applications. So don't procrastinate!

Create a checklist of application deadlines and use a calendar program like Google Calendar (calendar.google.com) or Microsoft Outlook, or a PDA, to get organized. Set reminders at least two weeks before the due date and display the calendar in an agenda-style view to plan your work. Highlight the scholarship programs that are your top priorities. The Fastweb scholarship site will also send you email reminders a few weeks before each set of deadlines.

The checklist should include all of the required supplemental materials — such as essays, recommendations and the FAFSA student-aid report — in addition to the application itself. It is not uncommon for a student to send the basic application in on time, only to miss the deadline for one or more supporting items.

Note whether the application deadline is a postmark or receipt deadline. If the latter, you will need to mail the application materials at least one week before the deadline date.

Start working on your applications as soon as possible. Don't wait until the last minute. If you are rushed, you won't have the opportunity to proofread the application as carefully.

Put each application's materials in a separate file folder. If there are several loose pages, label each page with your name and possibly also a page number. This will prevent parts of your application from getting lost or out of order. Attach a checklist to the front of the folder listing all the required materials and the date you requested and sent the materials. The checklist should also indicate the deadlines.

Also keep a master checklist of all the scholarships to which you are applying, so you can check off the completion of each application.

Create an Accomplishments Resume

An accomplishments resume, sometimes called a portfolio, is a one-page summary of your most significant activities, interests, hobbies, awards and accomplishments. It should focus on the most impressive and relevant accomplishments. This can be a useful tool for completing applications. Sometimes you can include a copy with your application. However, even if you have a lot of impressive accomplishments, the selection committee is unlikely to read beyond the first page, so keep it to just one page.

Do not include your Social Security number in your accomplishments resume. Your Social Security number is private information that should be provided only to organizations that have a legitimate need to know. Otherwise, you are increasing the risk of identity theft.

After you've compiled your accomplishments resume, ask your parents to review it. They may identify a few strengths and activities that you may have overlooked.

The accomplishments resume not only helps you complete applications; it's also a form of self-discovery. To see where you're headed in the future, you have to know where you are now and where you've been in the past. Recurring themes can be a sign of your primary interests. What do you enjoy doing? What are you good at? What subjects do you find the most interesting and exciting?

Tailor Your Application to the Sponsor's Goals

Identify the scholarship sponsor's goals and tailor your application to fit. Why are they sponsoring this scholarship? What are they looking for in an applicant? Many scholarship programs mention the selection criteria in the application materials. Also do a little background research on the sponsor. Look for the sponsor's mission statement on their web site, often in the "about us" section of the site.

Sponsors may have a variety of goals in offering a scholarship. Some companies offer scholarships as a form of community development, to invest in the future of the communities where they are based. Others offer scholarships to help retain current employees and recruit future employees. Most large employers offer some form of tuition assistance. Colleges may offer scholarships to recruit a talented and diverse student body. Colleges may also offer scholarships in specific majors to encourage students to enroll in underrepresented fields (e.g., scholarships for women and minorities to pursue majors in science and engineering and men to pursue majors in library science). Membership organizations tend to offer scholarships to promote their field or the mission of the organization. Other scholarships may be established to honor the memory of someone who has passed away by providing a legacy that perpetuates his or her values.

To increase your chances of winning a scholarship, highlight those aspects of your background that match the sponsor's mission, goals and selection criteria. Try critiquing your application from the sponsor's perspective.

It helps if you have a strong background in an area that is relevant to the scholarship sponsor's goals. What have you accomplished in that area?

Depth is often more important than breadth, especially if it is in an area of importance to the sponsor. Most sponsors are seeking excellence in some area. Quality is more important than quantity.

Do not lie or exaggerate on the application form. There's a difference between tailoring your application to highlight relevant aspects of your background and fabricating inaccurate statements. If there are inconsistencies and discrepancies, you will not make the final selection.

Even stretching the truth can hurt your application. For example, if you list photography as a hobby on an application for a science scholarship, don't be surprised if you're asked to explain the chemical reactions that make photography possible (or the difference between CCD and CMOS sensors in digital photography) during your interview.

Read and Follow the Instructions

Scholarship sponsors are often quite rigid in filtering out any applicants who don't follow the instructions or who miss the deadlines. They will also eliminate any applications that do not strictly satisfy the stated requirements. Some will even eliminate applications with spelling and grammar errors.

These steps are usually performed by clerical staff, not the selection committee. Evaluating applications is time-consuming, so the sponsor tries to avoid wasting committee time on applications that are incomplete or that don't follow the instructions. There are more than enough qualified applications that followed the rules. Moreover, if you can't follow a few simple application instructions, it doesn't bode well for your academic performance and success in college.

Make Your Application Stand Out

Try to make your application distinctive and memorable. Too many scholarship applications are boring, with nothing to distinguish them from other applications. After a selection committee member has read about two dozen applications, they start to blur together. To increase your chances of winning, do something different that will help your application stand out from all the rest. Give the selection committee a (positive) reason to remember your application.

Take a step back and ask yourself whether the real you is captured by your application. Do the words leap off the page with fire and power or do they just describe a generic student? The essay *must* say something about you that can't be figured out from your background resume. Make it personal. A good place to start is with your passions, since that often leads to a more interesting application. What excites you?

While overcoming genuine adversity or achieving something significant can yield a memorable application, you do not need to have an extreme experience to prepare an interesting application. Ordinary, everyday experiences can be memorable if they provide insights into your personality and your hopes and dreams. Keeping a diary can sometimes help you identify interesting essay topics.

Quality is more important than quantity, as mentioned earlier. Do not submit extra essays or video clips. Try to distill your essence in the application. Make every word count.

Avoid gimmickry. There are no shortcuts to an interesting application. Almost every unique idea you can think of has been done before, hundreds of times. Pop-up applications, poetry and word paintings are not new ideas. Don't write your essay in crayon or magic marker. Don't write about your dead dog, your cluttered desk or your favorite artist. Write about quirkiness only if you are an oddball.

If you write about a life-changing experience, you should focus on how it changed your behavior and not as much on how it changed your perspective. What are you doing differently now as a result of this experience?

There are two ways to make an application memorable, the right way and the wrong way. Make sure your application stands out in a positive manner. A negative event might be memorable, but it will reduce your chances of winning. For example, while the selection committee will certainly remember an essay about cheating on a test or engaging in an illegal activity, they will question your integrity and will be unlikely to award you a scholarship.

Likewise, the application should be in good taste. That doesn't mean including a batch of homemade cookies or candy (a trite gimmick), but rather omitting anything that is likely to offend or disgust the reviewers of your application. For example, an essay about slaughterhouses may be offensive to vegetarians. When in doubt, leave it out.

Avoid topics that are likely to be polarizing or that generate extreme opinions. These include religion, politics, abortion, sexual orientation, same-sex marriage, gun control, capital punishment, animal experimentation, creationism, global warming and illegal immigration, for example. An essay on one of these topics may be memorable, but if the reader disagrees with your position on the issue, you won't win the scholarship. A primary exception to this rule is when the topic speaks to the purpose of the scholarship competition.

Ask to Be Nominated

Some scholarships require that you be nominated by your school or the local chapter of a national organization. It is not possible to apply directly for these scholarships. But that doesn't mean you can't improve your chances of winning.

If a scholarship requires a nomination, find out who is responsible for nominating applicants and ask them to nominate you (politely). Often the nominator will not have a formal process for selecting a nominee. If the nomination deadline is approaching, sometimes they will nominate you simply because you're the only one who asked. Otherwise, your name will be added to the list of students under consideration for a nomination.

When you ask to be nominated, bring a copy of your accomplishments resume to give to the nominator along with the nomination forms. Include a list of important information such as the deadline date and a one-paragraph summary of what the scholarship sponsor is seeking. It is also polite to provide the nominator with a stamped and addressed envelope.

After you are nominated, send a thank-you letter to the nominator.

Write a Winning Scholarship Essay

Don't skip essay contests. They aren't as much work as you might fear. You can reuse essays in subsequent scholarship applications to save time, but tailor and tweak the essay to each application. Reusing an essay lets you improve it with each revision.

If you have trouble writing essays, try talking out loud. Record yourself as you talk and then transcribe the recording. Most people can speak (and think) much faster than they can print or type (150–200 words per minute vs. 20–40 words per minute), so speaking is less likely to interfere with your flow of thoughts. It's also a good way of avoiding writer's block.

Use an outline to provide your essay with structure and to focus and organize your thoughts. Too many application essays are written in a stream-of-consciousness style, jumping from point to point and failing to connect one thought to another. Using an outline will allow you to present your arguments and ideas in a manner that supports your conclusions, yielding a more powerful essay. If you write the outline after you've written the first draft of the essay, it can help you structure the essay as you edit it.

Give examples and be specific. Avoid vagueness and generalities. Support your claims with evidence and concrete details so the reader can draw his or her own conclusions. For example, if you say that one of your best qualities is leadership, give an example of a time when you demonstrated leadership. Similarly, a question about community service should not be answered with a vague "I like helping others and feel that it is important," but rather should include specific examples of how you have helped others.

Providing examples can have a big impact on whether you win the award. If your application is filled with vague and abstract answers, the selection committee will find it difficult to evaluate your qualifications. Selection committees rarely accept an applicant's self-evaluation at face value. If you provide them with specific, concrete examples, they will form their own opinions and cite your experiences and accomplishments as evidence in support of those opinions.

Pick a Good Essay Topic

The most common essay questions ask about your background, your major influences, your role models, your academic plans (or intended field of study), your personal accomplishments and hobbies, your participation in volunteer and community-service activities and your future goals. Other common topics include current events, social issues and overcoming adversity.

The essay questions included in the Common Application[6] illustrate some of the more common essay questions:

Evaluate a significant experience, achievement, risk you have taken, or ethical dilemma you have faced and its impact on you.

Discuss some issue of personal, local, national or international concern and its importance to you.

Indicate a person who has had a significant influence on you, and describe that influence.

Describe a character in fiction, a historical figure or a creative work (as in art, music, science, etc.) that has had an influence on you, and explain that influence.

A range of academic interests, personal perspectives and life experiences adds much to the educational mix. Given your personal background, describe an experience that illustrates what you would bring to the diversity in a college community, or an encounter that demonstrated the importance of diversity to you.

When looking for a good essay topic, focus on problems. Within every problem lurks a creative and interesting solution. Problems can also be a source of drama and conflict, which makes an essay more interesting. Write an essay about how you identified and solved a problem and the impact of your efforts. Better yet, talk about how you overcame personal adversity and how the experience affected you. This is much more interesting than typical essay topics such as

---

6   https://www.commonapp.org/CommonApp/DownloadForms.aspx

discussing a favorite author or an inspiring role model, because it is more deeply personal.

Personalize your essay. Be passionate about the topic. Talk about how the topic affected you and how you affected others. Feelings and emotions make for a more vivid essay. Take this opportunity to provide an insight into your background — an insight that can't be found in the rest of the application. Personal anecdotes yield a more interesting essay, as people are hardwired to listen to stories.

When you're asked a broad question or told to "tell us about yourself," respond by summarizing your relevant background and qualifications for the award. Remember, this is a competition, not a blind date. Highlight how you are the best candidate for the scholarship. But write a response that is more than just a mechanical reciting of facts and figures. Try telling a story using a personal experience or weave together a tapestry that connects your past to the present and your future goals. How did you become interested in the field? What contributions will you make? What is your promise as a future worker in the field?

Questions about leadership are more often about making a difference in the community and motivating others than about holding an impressive title. Describe your contributions and the impact of your efforts, especially any measurable outcomes. Talk about how you've helped other people and will continue to help them.

Be creative and original, but avoid humor and gimmickry. Originality and creativity in the essay count for a lot because too many essays are trite and boring. Avoid posturing and pretense, as exaggerated positions can annoy or even offend.

Avoid controversy, as it will prime the reader with negative thoughts. This will make the judge more likely to think about your application negatively.

Avoid philosophical essays. Few people have lived long enough or are insightful enough to develop a personal philosophy that isn't trite, superficial, preachy or tiresome.

If you are asked to write about your greatest weakness, do not try to characterize a strength as a weakness. Everybody has a few weaknesses, so sidestepping the question just insults the reader and demonstrates a lack of honesty. Instead, identify a real weakness and discuss the steps you have taken to address that weakness. The solution does not have to be perfect. For example, one of my weaknesses is a tendency to become more critical when I have a headache. I might write an essay along the following lines:

> I'm normally a very easygoing person, but I become irritable and less tactful when I'm starting to suffer from a migraine. To solve this problem I try to be more careful when I feel a migraine approaching. I can usually tell that I'm about to get a migraine about 2-3 hours in advance. I will hold my response to an email message until the next day and reread it before sending it. I avoid making any important decisions when I'm in pain. I also try to minimize my exposure to my migraine triggers, such as tobacco smoke or the smell of burnt coffee. When I travel, I insist on a smoke-free hotel room and hypoallergenic pillows. (I will not stay in hotels where the "no smoking" signs aren't permanently affixed to the walls, as those hotels often try to cheat.) Thankfully, I get migraines only about once a month these days.

Nobody will deny you a scholarship because you have a weakness, but the essay adds a human dimension and personality. It's an opportunity to demonstrate growth and self-knowledge. It makes you a more interesting, multidimensional person.

The same is true of essay questions that ask you to write about your biggest mistake. Many people try to avoid taking responsibility for causing an error because it might give the reviewer a bad impression. Picking a mistake that was not your fault or which was caused by circumstances beyond your control avoids giving a real answer. It tells the reviewer nothing about you as a person, other than your skill at avoiding the question or failing to take personal responsibility for your actions. It does not demonstrate your growth and maturity. You are human. You make mistakes. What matters is how you correct your mistakes and learn from them.

Essay DOs and DON'Ts

Read and follow the directions. Sometimes the directions can clarify the intent of the question. If you don't follow the directions, you will give the scholarship committee a negative impression, telling them that you can't or won't follow instructions.

Do not skip application questions. If a question does not apply to you, write "Not Applicable" or "N/A." Do not leave any question blank. An incomplete application will be rejected.

Use the inverted-pyramid writing style in your essays. The inverted-pyramid writing style lists the most important information first. Given the limited time available to review each application, the scholarship committee members may skim your application, reading just the first paragraph (or even just the first sentence) of your essays. You need to grab the reader's attention and communicate the most important information in the first paragraph. Get to the point and be concise. Do not ramble. Don't repeat information presented elsewhere in your application.

Be decisive and committed, not wishy-washy or tentative. When answering questions about why you chose a particular academic major, do not mention whether you are or were uncertain about your choice. If you are unsure about your path, why should a scholarship sponsor invest its money in your future? The scholarship sponsor wants to support students who will graduate with a degree in a particular academic major, not students who may switch to a different major or drop out entirely midway through the program.

Talk about something of interest to you. Tell a story. If you are passionate about a topic, it will be more interesting to the reader.

Do not pull an all-nighter to write the essay. You won't have enough time to reflect on and edit the essay, and the essay is likelier to be disjointed, disconnected, incoherent and full of errors.

Don't edit the life out of your essay. Imagine the tedium of reading thousands of boring student essays. Be memorable and interesting.

Don't have your parents write the essay for you. Don't let your parents rewrite the essay so much that there is more of them than you in the essay. Most judges can tell the difference between an essay written by a student and an essay written by a parent. Most people are not aware of the stylistic choices they make that are obvious signals that an essay was written by an adult and not a student.

If there is a word limit, adhere to it. Some scholarship sponsors will count the number of words in the essays and will disqualify an application even if it is just one word over the limit. Some online application forms will block you from submitting an essay if it is over the word limit and the online applications may count the number of words differently. So be prepared to edit the essay, if necessary. (Sometimes careful cutting of an essay to fit a word limit can improve the essay by eliminating unnecessary stray thoughts or wordiness.)

If there is a page limit, don't try to squeeze more text on a page by adjusting the font size and page margins. This can make the essay unreadable. Stick with standard 1-inch margins, 10 point or larger font size and normal line spacing. (If people can't read your essay because you used a tiny typeface, you won't win the scholarship.) Either indent the first line of each paragraph or leave a blank line between paragraphs. Use serif fonts like Times Roman or Century Schoolbook for the body copy and sans-serif fonts like Arial or Helvetica for headings and titles. Do not include gratuitous images just to break up the gray text — every image and table must inform the reader.

If your essay doesn't fit, edit it. Careful editing can often improve an essay by eliminating unnecessary verbiage.

Fellowship and Scholarship Applications Are Different

The word *fellowship* refers to a grant for advanced study or research, typically awarded to a graduate or professional student. This is in contrast with the word *scholarship* which refers to a merit-based grant typically awarded to an undergraduate student. An *assistantship* is an award of a full or partial tuition waiver and/or living stipend in exchange for teaching or research duties.

Applying for a graduate fellowship is a little different from applying for an undergraduate scholarship. Graduate school is much more focused on academics and the fellowship competitions tend to be more serious. College or institutional aid, including internal fellowships and teaching and research assistantships, is usually awarded by the graduate department and not a centralized financial aid office. Centralized financial aid offices are more common for undergraduate financial aid than for graduate and professional degree programs.

The essay question on a fellowship application is usually called a "personal statement." It will focus on your relevant background and your potential contributions to the field. The selection committee wants to understand your background in the field and how it will contribute to where you are headed. There is a lot more emphasis on your potential as a future worker in the field.

Doctoral degrees like the Ph.D. are research degrees, so evidence of your ability to conduct research will be a big plus. Students who have published an article in a peer-reviewed journal or presented their work at a refereed conference will have an advantage in fellowship competitions.

Letters of recommendation should include a letter from your academic adviser. If you've worked on a research project with a faculty member, it can help to ask him or her for a letter of recommendation. A letter from your employer is more of a mixed bag even if you've worked in an area that is relevant to your field of study, since your supervisor may not be able to evaluate your performance from an academic perspective.

Practice on a Copy of the Application Form

Make a photocopy of the application form and practice completing the copy first. This is a good way of making sure that your answers fit in the available space. If there's not enough space, it is better to be selective than to attach additional sheets.

If you have to choose which accomplishments to list on the application form, focus on your most significant accomplishments. Quality is more important than quantity. The scholarship committee may look at only the first three accomplishments, so it is important to prioritize the order of the accomplishments. First, focus on how well the accomplishment matches the sponsor's mission and goals, listing the most relevant accomplishments first. Second, consider the impact on the community. Third, concentrate on the uniqueness and selectivity of the accomplishment, such as how it sets you apart. Top in the nation is more impressive than top in your school. This order — first sponsor, second community, third you — highlights the accomplishments that are most relevant to winning the award. Finally, list the most recent accomplishments first.

Neatness counts. If you have to handwrite your answers on the form, use print, not longhand, unless the application requires longhand.

Managing Online Applications

More applications are being submitted online these days.[7] While this may save on postage and make it easier to apply to more awards, it also presents its own challenges.

It is rather frustrating to write the perfect essay, only to have a form submission error delete the text. Write the essay in a separate word processing program, so you can save a copy before you submit it. After you cut and paste the essay into the web form, review the text carefully. Some word processing software uses special characters for punctuation or line ending characters that don't translate well when pasted into an online form. Review and edit the pasted text if necessary, so your apostrophes don't turn into commas. Do not

---

7   A recently developed XML scholarship application data standard called ScholarSnapp will increase the number of scholarship programs accepting online scholarship applications.

assume that the text will line up in any particular way, as the formatting may change.

Create a separate folder in your email client for each scholarship application. This will make it easier to manage the correspondence associated with the scholarship program. You may be able to create mail filters that automatically file the correspondence in the correct folder. Flag important messages, especially any messages that are time-sensitive. Emailing notes and ideas to yourself can help you capture fleeting thoughts.

Before sending an email message, double check the recipient list. Email programs sometimes substitute the wrong recipient.

Do not use abbreviations and shorthand conventions in your email messages, such as "u" for "you" or smiley faces or emoticons like ";-)". Write full sentences in proper English with correct capitalization and punctuation. Omit quotations and fancy diagrams from the signature section of the email message.

Proofread Your Applications

Proofread your application and essays, as spelling and grammar errors do not give a good impression.

The spelling and grammar correction tools included in word processing software catch some but not all errors. They cannot correct homophone errors such as it's/its, their/there/they're and principal/ principle. They also cannot correct other valid word spelling errors such as from/form.

It sometimes helps to print out a copy of your essay. It is easier to catch errors when reading on paper than on a vertical computer monitor. Try setting the font size to at least 11 point and the font to a serif face like Times Roman, as you will be more likely to overlook an error when it is printed in tiny type.

Read the essay aloud to see if it flows well.

Also ask a parent or teacher to read your essays, since one of the best ways of finding errors is to use a second set of eyeballs to review your work.

It is also important to keep the essay simple. Clarity is more important than a sophisticated writing style. Avoid run-on sentences. Limit each sentence to a single thought. Don't use big words. Overusing synonyms does not compensate for a weak essay, especially if you use a word inappropriately. The purpose of a thesaurus is to help you choose the right word, not to substitute a synonym for a repeated word. Don't use emoticons (smiley faces) or instant-messaging slang and acronyms. Avoid clichés or famous quotes as these are often signs of superficial thinking.

Use active voice, not passive voice. For example, write "This analysis influenced public policy" instead of "Public policy was influenced by this analysis." Active voice is more powerful, direct, concise and easier to comprehend. Passive voice is weaker and less committed. Good examples of action verbs for use in a scholarship application include:

analyzed, built, checked, coached, collected, compared, compiled, completed, conducted, conserved, coordinated, counseled, created, decided, defined, demonstrated, described, designed, developed, directed, discovered, drafted, edited, educated, enabled, encouraged, established, estimated, evaluated, executed, explained, fixed, founded, generated, guided, helped, identified, implemented, improved, increased, influenced, informed, initiated, inspired, installed, integrated, invented, judged, launched, led, maintained, managed, monitored, motivated, negotiated, observed, offered, operated, organized, performed, persuaded, planned, played, predicted, prepared, presented, printed, produced, promoted, proposed, published, recruited, repaired, researched, resolved, restored, retrieved, reviewed, served, sold, solved, studied, summarized, supervised, supported, taught, tested, trained, united, worked

Read *The Elements of Style.* by William Strunk Jr. and E.B. White for additional examples of active and passive voice.

Ask for a Great Letter of Recommendation

Many scholarships require one or two letters of recommendation. You can ask teachers, coaches, professors, advisors, employers, guidance counselors or the director of a community service activity where you volunteered your time to write you a letter. A great letter of recommendation can help your application stand out, helping you win the scholarship.

A recommendation by an independent, disinterested third party counts more than potentially biased sources such as relatives. Never include letters of recommendation from family members.

The purpose of the letter of recommendation is to provide the selection committee with third-party documentation and validation of your background. They want to read the opinion of someone who is familiar with your background and knows you well. It is even better if they can compare you with other students, especially students who have won the award previously.

When you talk to your recommenders, don't just ask whether they are willing to write you a letter of recommendation, but whether they are willing to write you a *great* letter of recommendation. Nobody likes having to write a lukewarm letter of recommendation, so give them an out. You want someone who can not only write well, but write well about you and praise you.

The recommendation should be relevant to the scholarship program. Don't submit a letter from your English teacher to a science scholarship competition, even if she writes well.

All else being equal, it is better to ask someone who has known you longer and who is more impressed by your qualifications. They can compare your performance with other students.

You can ask the same recommender to write a letter of recommendation for more than one scholarship application, if the recommender is relevant to the scholarship program. Once they've written one letter of recommendation on your behalf, writing the second letter is much easier. The previous recommendation can be tweaked slightly to fit each new scholarship program.

Do not be surprised if one of the people you ask to write a letter of recommendation asks you to write the first draft of the letter. He or she will then edit what you write and sign it. (This is more likely to occur at the college level than in high school.) Writing a good letter of recommendation is very difficult, especially if you're writing your own letter of recommendation.

Don't submit extra letters of recommendation unless the letters provide additional information and insights, and only in truly exceptional cases. If the instructions specifically prohibit the inclusion of extra letters of recommendation, don't submit an extra letter. At best, they will discard the extra letter. At worst, they will disqualify your application for a failure to follow instructions.

Give your recommenders a copy of your accomplishments resume. They will incorporate some of the details into their letter, making it seem as though they know you better than they do.

Also give the recommender a one-page summary of the scholarship, including the purpose of the award, the sponsor's goals and other important details. Summarize your relevant background that demonstrates how you fit the award. This will help the recommender customize his or her letter and make a better case for you to win the scholarship. The summary should also prominently mention the deadline for submitting the recommendation.

Provide the recommender with a stamped and addressed envelope and all required forms, as noted previously.

Ask the recommender to write the letter at least four weeks before it is due. Gently remind them ten days before the deadline, asking them whether they have mailed the recommendation yet or need more information from you.

Waive your rights to read the recommendation. Selection committees view such letters as more candid and informative.

Send the writer a thank you note after the letter has been mailed. You will probably ask them to write additional letters for you in the future. If you send them a thank you, it will give them a good impression and make them more willing to spend time helping you.

Practice for the Scholarship Interview

Most scholarship programs do not include an interview as part of the selection process. But if there is an interview, it often carries a lot of weight in choosing the scholarship recipients.

If you want to ace the scholarship interview, practice, practice, practice. The more you practice, the less nervous you will be during an actual interview. Ask your parents or a friend to conduct mock interviews. Good questions for practice interviews include questions about your background, academic achievements, hobbies, extracurricular activities, academic and career goals, upbringing and values, as well as any notable awards and activities. Videotape the mock interview, so you can see how you respond to questions. You will be shocked at all your *ums*, *ahs* and twitches.

Be Professional During the Scholarship Interview

Don't be late to the interview. Arrive at least 15 minutes before the scheduled interview.

Visit a restroom before the interview. Brush your teeth with a tooth brush and toothpaste. Shave before the interview. Shower the morning of the interview and use deodorant.

Do not drink caffeinated beverages before or during the interview. If the interviewer offers you something to drink, ask for a glass of water, but sip it sparingly.

Dress appropriately. Use a mirror to check your appearance before arriving for the interview. Wear shoes, not flip-flops. Wear modest clothing with a clean, professional appearance. Business attire, such as a suit, is best. A sweater is ok if you don't own a suit. Do not wear silk-screened or tie-dyed shirts. Do not wear cutoff jeans or clothing with holes or tears in it. Do not wear plaid. Remove extraneous jewelry — wear at most one set of earrings and show no other visible body piercings. Cover any tattoos if possible.

Pay attention when the interviewer tells you his or her name. There's nothing more embarrassing than forgetting the name of the interviewer. If you pay attention to the name and use it soon after you hear it, you're more likely to remember it. Use their name formally, "Mr. XYZ" or "Ms. ABC" or "Dr. PQR" or "Prof. LMN." Do not use their first name as that is too informal. While there are tricks you can use if you forget someone's name — such as asking "How do you spell your name?" — these tricks can sometimes backfire ("S M I T H").

If it seems appropriate, ask the interviewers for their business cards. This can help you remember their names and give you the addresses for sending a thank-you note. Do not pick your teeth with the business cards or otherwise play or fidget with them.

Be polite. Use all the good manners your parents taught you. Introduce yourself with a firm handshake. Say "thank you" and "please." Say "yes," not "yeah." Be neat and tidy. Smile (but only if it doesn't look like a grimace). Make eye contact but don't stare. Do not chew gum, eat, fart or smoke in front of the interviewers. Sit up straight in your chair and do not slouch. Do not bite or chew your nails. Do not pick your nose.

If the interview is over lunch or dinner, practice proper table manners. Order a light, inexpensive meal and avoid food that is messy. Do not drink soda or other carbonated beverages, as burping is considered rude. Do not drink alcohol. Do not speak with your mouth full. Start with the outermost utensils first. Use a fork and knife to eat the food, not your fingers. Do not clean your teeth with the napkin.

If the interviewer asks if you have any questions, it's an opportunity to ask the interviewer about himself/herself, such as what interested them in this field or what they see as the most important challenges. (Do not ask personal questions.) Do not waste this opportunity, as the interviewer will form a more positive impression of you if you are genuinely interested in what they have to say. People like to talk about themselves. Being a good listener is as important as knowing all the answers to their questions. Also ask them if they have any advice for you.

Send a personalized thank-you note after the interview to each person who interviewed you. Very few students say thank you these days, so sending a thank-you note will give a good impression.

React Calmly to Challenging Interviews

Some interviewers will deliberately try to challenge you to see how well you handle an uncomfortable situation. Most interviews are polite and conversational, but you might encounter the rare confrontational interview. Such an interviewer might interrupt you while you are speaking and criticize your response. It's all about provoking a reaction. The interviewer wants to see how well you think on your feet. Do not take the bait. Do not let the stress get to you. React calmly.

Wait a few seconds before responding to any question, so you have some time to think before you speak. If you pause briefly before every question, it won't seem as odd when you need the time to think before responding. This is a useful technique even in non-confrontational interviews.

The interview should be a conversation, not an interrogation. Try to respond with more than just a yes or no to questions. The best interviews flow well from topic to topic, as opposed to being a series of disconnected questions.

Try to give positive responses, not negative responses. Positive responses will prime the interviewer to write a more positive assessment of your interview.

If you don't know the answer to a question, say so. The interviewers will be able to tell if you're trying to finesse or bluff your way through the answer. Remember, the interviewers have more experience interviewing candidates than you have being interviewed.

Sometimes the interviewers will deliberately ask you questions they are sure you don't know how to answer. They want to see how you respond to a difficult challenge. Do you give up or do you persist? Do you try to decompose it into easier and simpler sub-problems? Do you approach the problem with creativity? For example, in the Intel Science Talent Search competition, the judges ask a series of questions of increasing difficulty until they find a question that is beyond your level of expertise. They might start off asking about the closest star to the planet Earth (most people answer Alpha Centauri even though Sol, the sun, is the closest star), then about the distance of Alpha Centauri from Earth (4.3 light years), then what a light year is (the distance light travels in a year), then what the speed of light is (roughly 300,000 kilometers or 186,000 miles per second) and then how you would measure the speed of light (the Michelson and Morley experiment). The judges want to identify students who have the greatest potential as future researchers and this requires understanding each candidate's reaction to unsolved problems.

The judges at the Intel Science Talent Search may also ask questions that might be testing more than is immediately apparent. For example, when I was interviewed as a finalist in this competition (then known as the Westinghouse Science Talent Search), Glenn Seaborg, the Nobel laureate, asked me for the name of the 54th element of the period table of the elements. I did not know the answer, as I had never memorized the periodic table of the elements. But I tried visualizing the table and used that to describe some of the properties of the element (e.g., a noble gas), until suddenly I started laughing uncontrollably. Dr. Seaborg's tie was a periodic table of the elements and element 54 was clearly visible as Xe (Xenon). He was a gentle giant with a great sense of humor.

A Few Tips for Interviews by Telephone or Webcam

Some scholarship providers will conduct semifinalist interviews by telephone or webcam, since conducting an in-person interview can be expensive. But a telephone or webcam interview is less personal and the sound quality can affect your ability to make a connection with the interviewer.

Tips for Telephone Interviews

Answer the call in a quiet room, not a room with a lot of background noise or distractions.

Use a corded phone, not a cordless phone or cell phone, as the call quality will be better. Do not use a speakerphone, as most speakerphones have unsatisfactory audio quality. Some speakerphones have an annoying echo. Others will have the speaker cut out when you are talking, blocking the interviewer. You do not want to make it difficult for the interviewer to hear you or talk to you.

Keep a single page of notes of key points in front of you, along with a copy of your accomplishments resume. One of the benefits of a telephone interview is that you can make yourself seem smarter if you prepare for the interview in advance. The interviewer won't know that you have a few notes in front of you. But the notes should be there to jog your memory. Do not read the notes out loud, as most people can tell the difference between a canned and a candid response.

Tips for Webcam Interviews

If the interview will be conducted using a webcam, clean the lens on your webcam before participating in the interview.

Place the webcam at eye level in the middle of the computer screen so that you will appear to be looking at the interviewer when you are looking at their video on the screen. If you can't control the placement of the webcam, look at the webcam during the interview instead of at the screen. Do not glance at the video of the interviewer, as this will give you a "shifty-eyed" look.

Review a snapshot of the image seen through the webcam to ensure that there are no embarrassing posters or other items in the background. Ideally the background should be uncluttered.

Final Steps Before You Submit Your Application

Double-check to make sure you aren't missing an important part of the application. Incomplete applications will be disqualified.

Use a professional email address, such as first.last@gmail.com. An email address like "hotmamma@maildomain.com", "cowgirl@maildomain.com" or "imaflirt@maildomain.com" is inappropriate. If your personal email address is too inappropriate to use, get a free Gmail account and set it up to forward email to your personal address. You can also configure your email client to retrieve email from the Gmail account. Be careful to respond to email using the professional email address and not your personal email address. Do not include quotes, word art or emoticons in your signature.

If you use social networking web sites like Facebook, clean up the content and remove anything inappropriate or immature. Some scholarship providers might come across or review your Facebook page by googling your name. Employers often review your web pages to determine whether you have good sense. An unprofessional Facebook page can make the difference between winning an award and losing it. It's a good idea to Google your own name to see what shows up in the search results.

Make a photocopy of your complete application before mailing it. If your original application gets lost in the mail (or a secretary spills coffee on it), you can send them another copy. If you are submitting the application online, print out a copy of your application. (If you generate a PDF of your online submissions, keep a copy backed up on an archival storage medium such as a CD-ROM or USB drive. You may wish to also keep a paper copy since it is easier to scan through a printed document than to read the document on a vertical computer monitor.)

You will find it helpful to refer to old applications when you are working on applications for similar scholarship programs.

Pay attention to the deadlines. Note whether they are postmark or receipt deadlines. Mail your applications at least a week before the deadlines. Don't procrastinate. If you miss the deadline, your application will be disqualified. Keep a log of the date you mailed each application.

Send the applications by certified mail, return receipt requested, or with a certificate of mailing or delivery confirmation, or include a self-addressed stamped postcard that the sponsor can return to acknowledge receipt of the application materials.

If you send the applications through email, CC yourself on the message and file it in an email folder for the scholarship program. This will give you a record of when you sent the application.

Understand the Selection Process

Every scholarship selection committee operates differently, but there are some similarities. All involve a process of culling a large number of applications down to a much smaller set of finalists from whom the recipients are selected. Some use a computer program to make the first cut, while others have people perform the initial review. The selection process might involve volunteers, past winners or a set of industry professionals. Meetings might be face-to-face, by phone or mediated by an online tool. The following discussion reviews a typical selection process.

First, there will be a clerical review that will weed out the applications that do not satisfy the prerequisites. Incomplete applications that are missing required information will be disqualified, as will illegible and late applications. Applications that are unqualified will also be discarded. If the scholarship program requires a 3.5 GPA and you have a 3.4 GPA, your application will not be considered.

Usually the application will be scored along multiple dimensions, such as an academic dimension and an extracurricular or leadership dimension. The scores will be combined into an overall score by summing them (perhaps using a weighted sum to count one dimension more heavily). This allows a slight weakness in one area to be compensated for by strengths in other areas.

This scoring will be used to group the candidates into three categories: strong, moderate and weak. The weak candidates will not be subjected to any further review. The moderate and strong candidates will be subjected to a quick review, where committee members spend only a few minutes reading each application before making a snap determination of whether the application merits further consideration. After this first pass, the best applications will be subjected to a more in-depth read.

Committee members might be expected to pick their top ten candidates and then champion them in a face-to-face committee meeting. Some finalists will be easy, as they will be included in the top picks of all the committee members. Others will require some discussion. In some cases, two or three applications will be compared side-by-side. The final decision might depend on slight nuances.

Try to be unique and memorable so that the scholarship committee members will refer to you as "the student who _____" and not as just another applicant. This makes your application more prominent.

The scholarship committee might also distinguish between finalists according to the potential impact of the award on the finalist. Scholarship sponsors want to award their scholarships to students who, with the help of the scholarship, will succeed in college and obtain the degree. They want their money to make a difference. They want winners who will reflect well on the sponsor and make them proud.

PITFALLS AND DANGERS

There are a variety of pitfalls and other problems to avoid while pursuing scholarships.

Beware of Scholarship Scams

Unfortunately, there are many scams that try to take advantage of unsuspecting families who need help paying for college. In most cases, the scholarship scams will use a reasonable-sounding excuse to try to get money from you.

Here are several signs of a scam:

1. Beware of scholarships that charge application, processing or administrative fees, even if the fee is just a few dollars. Legitimate scholarships give out money, they do not collect money. If you have to pay money to get money, it's probably a scam. Never invest more than a postage stamp to get information about scholarships or to apply for scholarships.

2. Watch out for scholarship sites that guarantee that you will win a scholarship. Nobody can guarantee that you'll win a scholarship, as winning depends on your performance and the scholarship sponsor's selection committee. Such guarantees are clearly fraudulent.

3. Be careful about giving out your personal information, especially your bank account number, credit card number or Social Security number. Most legitimate scholarships do not ask for this information. Scam artists can use a demand draft to remove money from your bank account with just

your bank account number — they do not need a signed check to do this.

4. Use of the unclaimed-aid myth is another sign of a scam. The most common form of this myth is "$6.6 billion in scholarships went unclaimed last year." This myth is based on a 1976-77 academic-year study by the National Institute of Work and Learning which estimated that $7 billion was potentially available from employers for employees in the form of employer tuition assistance (if every employee were to go to college) but that only $300 million to $400 million was used each year. So this myth is based on a 30-year-old estimate that has never been substantiated and has nothing to do with scholarships. The only scholarships that go unclaimed are ones that can't be claimed, such as the scholarship for a Catholic student born with a last name of Zolp enrolled at Loyola University of Chicago. (You can't change your name to qualify.)

Avoid the Most Common Application Mistakes

The following are some of the most common mistakes on scholarship applications:

- Missing deadlines.

- Failing to proofread the application. Particularly egregious errors include typos in your name and the name of the scholarship sponsor.

- Failing to follow directions, especially with regard to the essay length or the number of recommendations.

- Omitting required information. Incomplete applications aren't considered and thus can't win.

- Applying for a scholarship for which you do not satisfy the eligibility requirements.

- Failing to apply for a scholarship for which you are eligible.

- Failing to customize the application to each program, especially if you mention the name of the wrong scholarship program in your essay.

- Writing a boring essay.

- Having parents do all the work. Paying for college should be a joint family effort.

Deal with Rejection

Rejection is part of the process of applying for scholarships. Don't get depressed if you don't win. Even top scholarship winners have many more rejections than successes. Persevere. Remember, scholarship selection committees evaluate applications, not applicants. The selection committee knows only what your application and supporting materials tell it.

Ask for the reviewer's comments. Some scholarship programs are willing to share them with you and the comments can be quite specific and helpful for future competitions. If you address the comments in subsequent applications to the same or other scholarship programs, it can help you win. For example, students who won honorable mentions in the NSF Graduate Research Fellowship as college seniors have won as first-year graduate students by fixing the problems noted in their previous year's application.

AFTER YOU WIN A SCHOLARSHIP

The following tips discuss things you need to do after you win a scholarship.

Negotiate the Displacement of Need-Based Financial Aid

Unfortunately, winning a scholarship sometimes results in a reduction in your need-based financial aid.

Federal law and regulations require that colleges reduce certain types of need-based student financial aid when the sum of need-based student aid, scholarships and grants exceeds financial need by more than $300. This is referred to as an *overaward*.

The types of federal student aid that can be reduced include the Federal Perkins loan, the subsidized Federal Stafford loan, Federal Work-Study and the Federal Supplemental Educational Opportunity Grant. The Federal Pell Grant, Academic Competiveness Grant and National SMART Grant cannot be reduced. Colleges can also reduce the aid they award using their own funds.

Since colleges have some flexibility in how they reduce aid, most will reduce their own aid before touching the federal aid.

So if you are receiving need-based financial aid, it is possible that winning a scholarship will not yield an increase in the total amount of financial aid you receive. Your net cost will likely remain unchanged.[8] However, many colleges will allow a scholarship to first

---

8   Net cost is the difference between the cost of attendance and the financial aid package, including outside scholarships and student loans. Most colleges have a similar net cost, about the same as the expected family contribution.

substitute for need-based loans, yielding a reduction in your out-of-pocket cost.[9]

Every college has an "outside scholarship policy" that dictates how a student's need-based financial aid package is reduced when the student receives a private scholarship. The best policies allow the scholarship to first eliminate any unmet need (i.e., fill the gap between financial aid and financial need) and second to replace self-help aid, such as need-based student loans and campus employment. This maximizes the financial benefit to the student. Others will allow the scholarship to replace self-help aid up to a threshold — $1,000 and $2,500 are the most common thresholds — and then reduce self-help and gift aid equally. Others reduce only gift aid after the threshold is met. The worst policies use the scholarship to replace only institutional grants, yielding no net financial benefit to the student.

Talented students who have won a lot of scholarships are sometimes able to negotiate a more favorable outside scholarship policy. You won't be able to get the college to increase the total amount of financial aid, but you might be able to get them to reduce loans before grants. Your goal is to reduce the loan and work burden as much as possible. You might be able to convince the college to increase the cost of attendance to shelter more of the scholarships, such as by adding the cost of a computer or other education-related expenses. You can also try using the funding you've earned to leverage non-financial benefits, such as working as a research assistant to a well-known professor, getting a more favorable work-study job or getting first pick of available dorm rooms (or entry into the honors dorm). Emphasize how the scholarship is important to you as a student and to the college as an institution, especially if the scholarship is prestigious.

---

9   Out-of-pocket cost is the difference between the cost of attendance and just scholarships and grants. It excludes student loans, which have to be repaid. The out-of-pocket cost corresponds to your bottom line cost to attend the college. The out-of-pocket cost can vary significantly from college to college.

If you've won several scholarships that together will result in an overaward, consider asking the scholarship sponsors to allow you to defer all or part of the scholarship to a future academic year. Also tell the scholarship sponsor about any displacement issues, such as the college reducing institutional grants by the amount of your scholarship while retaining a gap between financial need and financial aid, as the scholarship sponsor may be in a stronger position to convince the college to adopt a more favorable outside scholarship policy.

Keep Your Scholarship

After you've won a scholarship, find out whether it is renewable and review the conditions of the award.

If the scholarship is renewable, review the requirements for retaining eligibility. Often, you must be making satisfactory academic progress toward a degree — for instance, maintaining a minimum GPA. You may have to be enrolled full-time. You may be required to major in a particular academic field of study. Some scholarships require participation in community service or other activities.

Many scholarships require that you send a personalized annual letter with a progress report to the donor or to submit a renewal form, as well as a copy of your academic transcripts. It is easier to prepare a progress report if you keep a diary or log of your significant accomplishments as they occur.

If you win a major award or other recognition, tell the scholarship sponsor about it. Scholarship-granting organizations like to highlight noteworthy accomplishments of their scholars as a way of demonstrating the value of their programs. This helps them help future scholars. The Intel Science Talent Search web site, for example, talks about how the program's alumni (more than 2,600 finalists as of 2009) have received seven Nobel Prizes, two Fields Medals, ten McArthur Foundation Fellowships and a variety of other honors.

Understand the Taxability of Scholarships

Your scholarship might be taxable.

If you are a degree candidate and your scholarship or fellowship is used to pay for tuition and required fees, books, supplies and equipment, it will be untaxed, provided that the scholarship or fellowship is not awarded as compensation for services performed by the student. Any amounts used for room and board or other living expenses will be taxable.

Keep receipts for purchases of books, supplies and equipment. Often these items can be returned for a cash refund with a receipt and a store credit without a receipt. Some college bookstores require a receipt for all returns. Also, the textbook allowances included in the cost of attendance are estimates (often underestimates). If your costs are higher, keeping the receipts can help you reduce your tax liability.

If you are not a degree candidate, the full amount of your scholarships and fellowships will be taxable.

The full amount of your scholarships and fellowships are exempt from Social Security taxes (FICA) regardless of whether you are a degree candidate.

For additional details, see IRS Publication 970, *Tax Benefits for Education*, at www.irs.gov/pub/irs-pdf/p970.pdf.

MAXIMIZE ELIGIBILITY FOR NEED-BASED AID

This book discusses how to increase your chances of winning a scholarship, not how to maximize your eligibility for need-based financial aid. However, since scholarships are only a part of the plan for paying for college, it is important to review a few basic tips about need-based aid from the government and colleges. Some scholarship providers will require that you apply for federal and state aid to ensure that you get all the money to which you are entitled.

1. Submit the Free Application for Federal Student Aid (FAFSA) at www.fafsa.ed.gov. You (and your parents, if you are a dependent student) will need a PIN to electronically sign the form. Go to www.pin.ed.gov to get a PIN. This lets you apply for financial aid from the federal government, state government, all public colleges and most private colleges. Do not wait until you've filed your income tax returns or been admitted to a college to file the FAFSA. Submit it as soon as possible after January 1, as some states have very early deadlines for state grants. You can use your W-2 and 1099 statements and/or the last paystub of the year to estimate the figures reported on the FAFSA. You will have an opportunity to correct any errors later. Or better yet, complete your federal income tax return early. Call 1-800-4-FED-AID and visit www.collegegoalsundayusa.org for free help with completing the FAFSA.

2. If there are any unusual family financial circumstances — such as job loss or a drop in income, death of a wage-earner, high unreimbursed medical or dental expenses or unusually high childcare or eldercare costs — contact the college and ask for a "professional judgment" review. Some colleges

call this a "special circumstances review" or a "financial aid appeal." Any financial circumstances that changed from last year to this year or which distinguish your family from the typical family can be grounds for an appeal. One-time events, such as unusual capital gains, may also be considered. Provide the college financial aid office with a photocopy of independent third-party documentation of the unusual circumstances. College financial-aid administrators have the authority to make adjustments to data elements on the FAFSA if justified by documented unusual circumstances. The amount of the adjustment will be based on the financial impact of the unusual circumstances on the family. The financial-aid administrator's decision is final.

3. Most tips for maximizing aid eligibility do not have much of an impact on the financial-aid package. So before you get involved in fancy asset-shifting games, play what-if games with a need-analysis calculator such as the one on the FinAid site, www.finaid.org. For example, parent assets have such a small impact on aid eligibility that advice to pay down consumer debt may have only a minimal impact on your expected family contribution. (The advice to pay down debt might still be good advice from a personal finance perspective. If you're paying high interest rates on your credit cards but earning only a token amount of interest on your savings account, using the savings to pay off the credit cards can improve your overall financial picture. Paying off the credit cards is like getting a tax-free return on investment since you will no longer be paying interest on the debt at high credit card interest rates.)

4. Save in the parent's name, not the child's name. Fewer than 4% of all dependent students have any contribution from parent assets. The value of qualified retirement plans, the net worth of the family's principal place of residence and small businesses owned and controlled by the family are ignored by the federal need analysis formula. There is also an asset protection allowance that is based on the age of the

older parent. This shelters roughly $50,000 in parent assets for the typical family with college-age children (median age 48). Above this threshold any remaining assets are assessed according to a bracketed scale with a maximum rate of 5.64%. In contrast, dependent student assets are assessed at a flat rate of 20% without any asset protection allowance. So money in the child's name can have a negative impact on need-based aid eligibility. To correct this problem, move the child's money into a custodial 529 college savings plan. This is treated as though it were a parent asset in the federal need analysis formula.

College savings plans owned by other relatives, such as grandparents, aunts and uncles, are not reported as an asset on the FAFSA. (Such assets are reported as an asset of the beneficiary on the CSS/Financial Aid PROFILE form.) However, any distributions are reported as untaxed income to the beneficiary. This can have a more severe negative impact on eligibility for need-based aid than reporting the college savings plan as an asset on the FAFSA. It may be advantageous to change the account owner to the student or parent.

5. There are two important income thresholds in the federal need analysis formula, $50,000 and $30,000. If a dependent student's parents have an adjusted gross income (AGI) that is less than $50,000 *and* they either are eligible to file an IRS Form 1040A or 1040EZ or satisfy other requirements, such as eligibility for certain federal means-tested benefit programs, the student will qualify for the simplified needs test which disregards assets. If the student qualifies for the simplified needs test and the AGI is less than $30,000, the expected family contribution (EFC) will be automatically set to zero, qualifying the student for a maximum Federal Pell Grant.

6. Minimize capital gains the year before the child enrolls in college and every year until the child graduates. Need

analysis formulas are heavily weighted toward income and income is based on the prior year's income as reported on your federal income tax returns. Realizing capital gains artificially inflates your income and can have a huge impact on aid eligibility.

See www.finaid.org/maximize for additional tips on maximizing need-based aid eligibility.

KEY SCHOLARSHIP RESOURCES

Scholarship Search

www.fastweb.com

www.finaid.org/scholarships

www.finaid.org/websearch

Full-Tuition Academic Scholarships

www.finaid.org/academicscholarships

Scholarships for Average Students

www.finaid.org/average

Scholarships for Community Service

www.americorps.gov

www.finaid.org/volunteering

Scholarship Scams

www.finaid.org/scholarshipscams

www.ftc.gov/scholarshipscams

Free Application for Federal Student Aid (FAFSA)

www.fafsa.ed.gov

www.pin.ed.gov

www.collegegoalsundayusa.org

1-800-4-FED-AID (1-800-433-3243)

www.finaid.org/fafsa

Tax Benefits for Education

www.finaid.org/taxbenefits

www.irs.gov/pub/irs-pdf/p970.pdf

GLOSSARY

1040 Form, 1040A Form, 1040EZ Form – The 1040 is the federal individual income tax return, filed annually with the IRS on April 15.

1099 Form – The 1099 Form is used by business to report income paid to a non-employee. Banks use this form to report interest income.

ACT – American College Test (ACT) is one of two national standardized college entrance examinations used in the United States of America. The other is the SAT. The ACT is popular in the West and Midwest. Most universities require either the ACT or the SAT as part of an application for admission.

AGI – Adjusted Gross Income (AGI) is the total income from taxable sources reduced by a set of adjustments. It is the last line on the first page of the IRS Form 1040.

AP – The Advanced Placement (AP) Test is used to earn credit for college subjects studied in high school. The AP tests are offered by ETS in the spring. AP tests are scored on a scale from 1 to 5 (the best possible score).

Academic Scholarship – An academic scholarship is a scholarship based on academic performance, such as grades, standardized test scores and class rank.

Academic Transcript – See Transcript.

Academic Year – An academic year is the time period during which school is in session, consisting of at least 30 weeks of instructional time. The school year typically runs from the beginning of September through the end of May at most colleges and universities.

Accomplishments Resume – An accomplishments resume is a summary of a student's academic and extracurricular accomplishments and awards, often prepared to help with scholarship and college admissions applications and recommendations.

Active Voice – A sentence is written in active voice when the subject is the source of the action, as opposed to the recipient of the action. It is a stronger form of expression.

All-Nighter – An all-nighter occurs when a student stays up all night working on a project or assignment or cramming for a test. All-nighters are often counterproductive because performance suffers due to a lack of adequate sleep.

AmeriCorps – AmeriCorps is national service program established by the federal government. Student participants can earn education awards equal to up to the maximum Pell Grant for each year of service and may use these awards to pay for their education or repay student loans.

Assistantship – An assistantship is a form of student aid for graduate students. The two main types are teaching assistantships (TA) and research assistantships (RA), where the student performs teaching and research duties in exchange for a full or partial tuition waiver and/or a small living stipend.

Associate's Degree – An Associate's Degree two-year undergraduate degree.

Award Letter – An award letter is an official document issued by a school's financial aid office that lists all of the financial aid awarded to the student, including grants, loans and work-study.

Award Year – The federal award year for receipt of federal student aid runs from July 1 to June 30.

Bachelor's Degree – A Bachelor's Degree is a four-year undergraduate degree.

CCD – A Charge Coupled Device (CCD) is an integrated circuit with a two-dimensional array of light sensitive diodes used for optical imaging in digital cameras. CCD sensors have greater resolution and light sensitivity than CMOS sensors and are less susceptible to noise.

CMOS – Complementary Metal Oxide Semiconductor (CMOS) is an integrated circuit with a two-dimensional array of light sensitive transistors used for optical imaging in digital cameras. CMOS sensors can be fabricated on standard silicon production lines, making them less expensive than CCD sensors. CMOS sensors have lower power requirements (yielding a longer battery life) but have lower resolution and lower light sensitivity. Each pixel in a CMOS sensor can be read individually.

COA – The Cost of Attendance (COA) is the total cost of education for a year of college, including tuition, fees, room, board, textbooks, supplies, transportation and personal/incidental expenses.

CSS/Financial Aid PROFILE – The PROFILE form is an alternative need analysis form used by about 250 colleges for awarding their own financial aid funds.

Calendar Year – The calendar year runs from January 1 to December 31.

Certificate of Mailing – A certificate of mailing is proof of the date a piece of mail was presented to the U.S. Postal Service for mailing.

Certified Mail – Certified Mail provides the equivalent of both a Certificate of Mailing and Delivery Confirmation. Return Receipt is an option with Certified Mail to obtain a receipt upon delivery including the recipient's signature.

College Board – A nonprofit educational association of colleges, universities, educational systems and other educational institutions.

College-Controlled Award – A college-controlled scholarship is awarded by a college and is usually restricted to students enrolled at the college.

Common Application – The Common Application is a shared college admissions application used by more than 400 colleges. See www.commonapp.org.

Delivery Confirmation – Delivery confirmation is proof of the date and time a piece of mail was delivered to the recipient.

Displacement – Displacement refers to the practice in which a college reduces a student's need-based financial aid package when the student wins an outside scholarship. Federal overaward regulations require colleges to reduce the need-based financial aid package (but not the Pell Grant) when the student is over-awarded. However, the college has some flexibility in choosing the types of aid that can be reduced. Each college has an outside scholarship policy to specify how need-based aid is reduced when a student is over-awarded.

EFC – The Expected Family Contribution (EFC) is a measure of a family's financial strength. It is the amount of money the family is expected to be able to contribute to the student's education, as determined by the Federal Methodology need analysis formula approved by Congress. The EFC includes the parent contribution and the student contribution and depends on the student's dependency status, family size, number of family members in school, taxable and nontaxable income and assets. The difference between the COA and the EFC is the student's financial need and is used in determining the student's eligibility for need-based financial aid.

ETS – Educational Testing Service (ETS) is the company that produces and administers the SAT and other educational achievement tests.

Emoticon – Emoticons, also known as smiley faces, are representations of facial expressions using a sequence of characters. For example, ;-) is a representation of a winking face. (Look at it sideways.) Emoticons were invented in 1982 by Scott Fahlman, a professor of computer science at Carnegie Mellon University.

Endowment – An endowment is a collection of funds owned by an institution and invested to produce income to support the operation of the institution and its programs. Part of the income is added to the endowment as a hedge against inflation. Many educational institutions use a portion of their endowment income for financial aid. A school with a larger ratio of endowment per student is more likely to give larger financial aid packages.

Enrollment Status – A student's enrollment status specifies whether the student is a full-time or part-time student. Generally a student must be enrolled at least half-time (and in some cases full-time) to qualify for student financial aid.

Essay – Scholarship applications often require the applicant to answer one or more essay questions. The essay is short, usually anywhere from a paragraph to a page in length.

FAA – See Financial Aid Administrator.

FAFSA – The Free Application for Federal Student Aid (FAFSA) is a form used to apply for Pell Grants and all other need-based aid. As the name suggests, no fee is charged to file a FAFSA. The FAFSA is submitted online at www.fafsa.ed.gov.

FICA – FICA is an employment tax used to fund Social Security benefits and Medicare.

FWS – Federal Work-Study (FWS) provides undergraduate and graduate students with part-time employment during the school year. The federal government pays a portion of the student's salary, making it cheaper for colleges to hire the student. Eligibility for FWS is based on need. Money earned from a FWS job is not counted as income for the subsequent year's need analysis process.

Fastweb – Fastweb is the first, largest, most popular and most frequently updated free scholarship matching service. Fastweb is available online at www.fastweb.com.

Fellowship – A fellowship is a form of aid given to graduate students to help support their education. Some fellowships include a tuition waiver or a payment to the university in lieu of tuition. Most fellowships include a stipend to cover reasonable living expenses. Fellowships are a form of gift aid and do not have to be repaid.

FinAid – FinAid was one of the first free web sites about paying for college. It provides encyclopedic student financial aid information, advice and tools. FinAid is available online at www.finaid.org.

Finalist – A finalist is an applicant who has reached the last stage of a scholarship competition before the recipients are selected.

Financial Aid – Financial aid is money provided to the student and the family to help them pay for the student's education or which is conditioned on the student's attendance at an educational institution. Major forms of financial aid include gift aid (grants and scholarships) and self-help aid (loans and work).

Financial Aid Administrator – The Financial Aid Administrator (FAA) is a college employee who determines eligibility for and awards student financial aid. A college's financial aid administrator may sometimes be called a financial aid advisor or financial aid counselor.

Financial Aid Package – A financial aid package is the complete collection of grants, scholarships, loans and work-study employment from all sources (federal, state, institutional and private) offered to a student to enable them to attend the college or university. Note that unsubsidized Stafford loans and PLUS loans are not considered part of the financial aid package, since these financing options are available to the family to help them meet the EFC and eligibility is not based on financial need.

Financial Aid Safety School – A financial aid safety school is a school you are certain will admit you and which is inexpensive enough that you can afford to attend even if you get no (or very little) financial aid.

Financial Need – Financial need is the difference between the COA and the EFC, the gap between the cost of attending the school and the student's resources. The financial aid package is based on the amount of financial need. The process of determining a student's need is known as need analysis.

Fiscal Year – The federal government's fiscal year runs from October 1 to September 30.

Foundation – A foundation is a nonprofit organization often established for a charitable purpose.

GPA – A student's Grade Point Average (GPA) is the average of a student's grades, converted to a numeric scale. Most GPAs are reported on a 4.0 scale, where a 4.0 is an A, a 3.0 is a B and a 2.0 is a C. Some schools use a 5.0 scale for the GPA.

Gapping – Gapping is the practice of failing to meet a student's full demonstrated need. It results in unmet need.

Gazillion – A gazillion is a very large and unspecified indefinite number.

Gift Aid – Gift aid is financial aid, such as grants and scholarships, which does not need to be repaid.

Gimmick – A gimmick is a quirky attention-seeking element of an application that does not add any value or substance to the application.

Grant – A grant is a type of financial aid based on financial need that the student does not have to repay.

IB – International Baccalaureate.

IRS – Internal Revenue Service.

Institution – The word institution is often used as a synonym for college or university.

Internship – An internship is a part-time job during the academic year or the summer months in which a student receives supervised practical training in a their field. Internships are often very closely related to the student's academic and career goals and may serve as a precursor to professional employment. Some internships provide very close supervision by a mentor in an apprenticeship-like relationship. Some internships provide the student with a stipend, while others are unpaid.

Interview – The scholarship interview is an opportunity for a representative of the scholarship sponsor to ask questions of the applicant and evaluate them in a more personal, face-to-face environment.

Loan – An education loan is a form of financial aid that must be repaid, often with interest. Need-based loans usually involve lower interest rates or subsidized interest, where the government pays the interest while the borrower is enrolled in college.

Lucrative – Profitable, generous.

Matriculate – A student matriculates in college when he or she enrolls in college for the first time. A student who just started the freshman year in high school will matriculate in four years. A newborn baby will matriculate in approximately 17 years.

Means-Tested – A means-tested program is one where eligibility is based on financial need.

Merit-based Aid – Financial aid that is merit-based depends on the applicant's academic, artistic or athletic merit or some other criteria and does not depend on the existence of financial need. Merit-based awards use grades, test scores, hobbies and special talents to determine eligibility for scholarships.

Mibster – A mibster is someone who plays with marbles.

Minority – A minority student is from a small group that is underrepresented in a particular field of study or degree program.

Often the term 'minority' is used in reference to racial minorities, such as African-American, Hispanic or Native American students.

Myth – A myth is a false claim or story that is not historically valid.

NPSAS – The National Postsecondary Student Aid Study (NPSAS) is a large, statistically significant quadrennial survey conducted every four years by the National Center for Education Statistics (NCES) at the U.S. Department of Education. It examines how undergraduate and graduate students pay for college.

NSF – National Science Foundation

Need – See Financial Need.

Need Analysis – Need analysis is the process of determining a student's financial need by analyzing the financial information provided by the student and his or her parents (and spouse, if any) on a financial aid form. The student must submit a need analysis form to apply for need-based aid. Need analysis forms include the Free Application for Federal Student Aid (FAFSA) and the CSS/Financial Aid PROFILE.

Need-Based – Financial aid that is need-based depends on the applicant's financial situation. Most government sources of financial aid are need-based.

Negotiation – Negotiation is an attempt to persuade the college to provide a better need-based financial aid package. Most negotiation is professional judgment in disguise.

Net Cost – Net cost is the difference between the cost of attendance and the need-based financial aid package. It is generally similar to the Expected Family Contribution (EFC) except when the college practices gapping. It does not vary much from college to college. See Out-of-Pocket Cost for a related definition. Generally, families should evaluate college financial aid award letters using out-of-pocket cost, not net cost.

Nomination – A nomination proposes an applicant as a suitable candidate for an award and discusses the applicant's qualifications.

Out-of-Pocket Cost – Out-of-Pocket cost is the difference between the cost of attendance and just the grants and scholarships and other gift aid in the need-based financial aid package. It reflects the bottom line cost to the family, the amount the family will need to pay out of current and future resources, such as savings, income and loans. See Net Cost for a related definition. While net cost does not vary by much from college to college, out-of-pocket cost can vary significantly, based on how much of need is met with grants instead of loans. Some of the elite non-profit colleges that have adopted no loans financial aid policies have lower out-of-pocket costs than many public colleges. Generally, families should evaluate college financial aid award letters using out-of-pocket cost, not net cost.

Outside Scholarship – An outside scholarship is a scholarship that comes from sources other than the school and the federal or state government.

Outside Scholarship Policy – A college's outside scholarship policy specifies how the college reduces the need-based aid package when a student is over-awarded. Usually the colleges will use the outside scholarship first to fill the gap between need and aid and then to reduce loans and grants equally.

Overaward – If the sum of a student's need-based financial aid and scholarships exceeds the demonstrated financial need by more than $400, the student is over-awarded and the financial aid package must be reduced to compensate.

PDF – The Portable Document Format (PDF) is a common file format for sharing documents independent of the hardware or software platform. It was created by Adobe Systems in 1993. Supplemental documents in a scholarship application should be provided in PDF format to ensure that the scholarship sponsor can read the documents.

PIN – The Personal Identification Number (PIN) is a secret password used to confirm an applicant's identity. PINs may be used to electronically sign documents. See www.pin.ed.gov.

PJ – See Professional Judgment

PROFILE – See CSS/Financial Aid PROFILE.

PTA – Parent Teacher Association.

Packaging – The process of assembling a financial aid package.

Passive Voice – A sentence is written in passive voice when the subject is the recipient of the action, as opposed to the source. It is a weaker form of expression.

Pell Grant – The Pell Grant is the largest need-based federal college grant program.

Pop – See Soda.

Postmark Date – The postmark date is the data a letter was mailed. Some scholarship deadlines are based on the postmark date and others are based on the receipt date.

Postsecondary – Postsecondary education is education beyond high school at the undergraduate, graduate or professional level.

Prestigious – The word prestigious means respected, influential, well-regarded, having an excellent reputation.

Prioritize – Prioritization is the process of listing a group of items or tasks in order of importance.

Procrastinate – To procrastinate is to delay, to postpone, to wait until the last minute. Students who procrastinate on their scholarship and college admissions applications are more likely to miss the deadlines. Procrastination is often caused by stress, anxiety, laziness or a lack of enthusiasm.

Professional Judgment – For need-based federal aid programs, the financial aid administrator can adjust the EFC, adjust the COA or change the dependency status (with documentation) when extenuating circumstances exist. For example, if a parent becomes unemployed, disabled or deceased, the FAA can decide to use estimated income information for the award year instead of the actual income figures from the base year. This delegation of authority from the federal government to the financial aid administrator is called Professional Judgment (PJ). Applicants who have unusual financial circumstances (such as high medical expenses, loss of employment or death of a parent) that affect their ability to pay for their education, should ask the financial aid administrator for a professional judgment review, sometimes called a special circumstances review or a financial aid appeal.

Proofread – Proofreading a document involves reviewing the document for logical, structural, spelling, punctuation and grammar errors.

Reaching School – A reaching school is a college that a student would love to attend, but which may be beyond the student's reach. Every student should apply to at least one reaching school in case the student has misjudged his qualifications for admission. See also Safety School.

Receipt Date – The receipt date is the date a letter was received. Some scholarship deadlines are based on the postmark date and others are based on the receipt date. Applications should be mailed to the sponsor at least a week before the deadline if the deadline is the date of receipt.

Recommendation – A letter of recommendation endorses a student's application for a scholarship or college admission.

Rejection – A scholarship application is rejected when the applicant is not selected for receipt of the scholarship.

Renewable Scholarships – A renewable scholarship is a scholarship that is awarded for more than one year. Usually the student must maintain certain academic standards to be eligible for subsequent years of the award. Some renewable scholarships will require the student to reapply for the scholarship each year; others will just require a report on the student's progress to a degree.

Research Assistantship – A research assistantship (RA) is a form of financial aid awarded to graduate students to help support their education. Research assistantships usually provide the graduate student with a waiver of all or part of tuition, plus a small stipend for living expenses. As the name implies, an RA is required to perform research duties. Sometimes these duties are strongly tied to the student's eventual thesis topic.

Resume – A resume is a summary of an applicant's relevant education, experience, activities and awards.

SAR – See Student Aid Report

SASE – Self-addressed stamped envelope.

SAT – The Scholastic Assessment Test (SAT) is one of the two national standardized college entrance examinations used in the U.S. The other is the ACT. The SAT (previously known as the Scholastic Aptitude Test) is administered by the Educational Testing Service (ETS). Most universities require either the ACT or the SAT as part of an application for admission.

STEM – STEM is an acronym for Science Technology Engineering and Mathematics.

Safety School – A safety school is a college that will almost certainly admit the student. The college admissions process is not predictable. Even "sure admits" are sometimes rejected. Some students are admitted to all the schools to which they apply; others are rejected by all the schools. Students should apply to at least one safety school to ensure that they are admitted to at least one college. See also Reaching School.

Satisfactory Academic Progress – A student must make satisfactory academic progress (SAP) in order to continue receiving student financial aid. Federal aid eligibility requires the student to have at least a 2.0 GPA and to be on track toward graduation within 150% of the normal timeframe for completion.

ScholarSnapp – ScholarSnapp is an XLM scholarship application data standard intended to facilitate electronic scholarship applications. See www.scholarsnapp.org.

Scholarship – A scholarship is a form of financial aid given to undergraduate students to help pay for their education. Most scholarships are restricted to paying all or part of tuition expenses, though some scholarships also cover room and board. Scholarships are a form of gift aid and do not have to be repaid. Many scholarships are restricted to students in specific courses of study or with academic, athletic or artistic talent.

Self-Help Aid – Self-help aid is financial aid in the form of loans and student employment. If every financial aid package is required to include a minimum amount of self-help aid before any gift aid is granted, that level is known as the self-help level.

Smiley Face – See emoticon.

Soda – Soda is a sweetened carbonated beverage. Popular brands include Coca-Cola, Pepsi, Sprite and Dr. Pepper.

Soda Pop – See Soda.

Soft Drink – See Soda.

Student Aid – See Financial Aid

Student Aid Report – The Student Aid Report (SAR) summarizes the information submitted on the FAFSA and provides the Expected Family Contribution (EFC).

Student Budget – See Cost of Attendance (COA).

Student Financial Aid – See Financial Aid

Teaching Assistantship – A teaching assistantship (TA) is a form of financial aid awarded to graduate students to help support their education. Teaching assistantships usually provide the graduate student with a waiver of all or part of tuition, plus a small stipend for living expenses. As the name implies, a TA is required to perform teaching-related duties.

Transcript – A transcript is a listing of the courses attempted and completed by the student, along with the grades achieved in the courses and an overall GPA.

Unmet Need – In an ideal world, the financial aid office would be able to provide each student with the full difference between their ability to pay and the cost of education. Due to budget constraints the financial aid office may provide the student with less than the student's demonstrated financial need. This gap is known as the unmet need.

W-2 Form – The W2 form lists an employee's wages and tax withheld. Employers are required by the IRS to issue a W2 form for each employee before February 28.

Webcam – A webcam is a digital camera connected to a computer and used to transmit video and still images over the Internet.

Wishy-Washy – An applicant is wishy-washy when he or she is undecided and lacks commitment or certainty.

TOP TEN LISTS

Talk show hosts like David Letterman have popularized the use of top ten lists, so it is only fitting that the David Letterman scholarship appear on the first of the following top ten lists of scholarships.

Top Ten Most Unusual Scholarships

1. Scholarship for Left-Handed Students

   The only scholarship for left-handed students is the Frederick and Mary F. Beckley Scholarship of up to $1,000. This scholarship is awarded to left-handed students who are enrolled at Juniata College (www.juniata.edu). For more information, write to Office of Student Financial Planning, Juniata College, 1700 Moore Street, Huntington, PA 16652.

2. Duck Brand Duct Tape Stuck at Prom Contest

   The Duck Brand Duct Tape Stuck on Prom Contest is open to students age 14 years or older who are attending a high school prom in the spring. U.S. citizenship is required. Entrants must enter as a couple (two individuals) and attend a high school prom wearing complete attire or accessories made from duct tape. The submission must include a color photograph of the couple together in prom attire. The first place prize consists of a $3,000 scholarship for each member of the winning couple and a $3,000 cash prize to the school that hosted the prom. Other prizes include $2,000 for second place, $1,000 for third and $500 for runners up. The winning couple will be selected based on a variety of criteria, including originality, workmanship, quantity of duct tape used, use of colors and creative use of accessories. The Duck Tape contest web site, www.stuckatprom.com/contests, includes photographs of the winning costumes in addition to application information and materials.

3. David Letterman Telecommunications Scholarship

The David Letterman Scholarship was established by David Letterman in 1985 to provide scholarships for telecommunications students at Ball State University (www. bsu.edu). The awards are intended for average students who nevertheless have a creative mind. Winners are selected primarily based on creativity. Projects may involve a variety of media, including written work, research, audio, video, graphics and film. The winner receives a $10,000 scholarship. The first runner-up receives $5,000. The second runner-up receives $3,333.

4. Zolp Scholarships

Your last name could be worth some money for college, if it happens to be Zolp. The Zolp Scholarship is restricted to students at Loyola University in Chicago (www.luc.edu/finaid) who are Catholic and whose last name is Zolp. The student's last name must appear on their birth certificate and confirmation certificate. The scholarship provides full tuition for four years.

There are many other "named" scholarships established by alumni at other colleges. These include scholarships for students with a last name of Scarpinato at Texas A&M University; Gatling[10] or Gatlin at North Carolina State University; and Baxendale, Hudson, Thayer, Downer or

---

10   Contrary to what has been reported in newspapers, this scholarship has no relationship to Richard Jordan Gatling, the inventor of the Gatling machine gun. The scholarship was endowed by John Gatling, who made his fortune as a real estate developer in Raleigh, North Carolina.

Bright at Harvard University. If your last name is Van Valkenburg or one of several variations and you are a descendant of Lambert and Annetje Van Valkenburg, who emigrated to the U.S. in 1643, you may be entitled to a $1,000 scholarship.

5. Patrick Kerr Skateboard Scholarship

The Patrick Kerr Skateboard Scholarship awards one $5,000 and three $1,000 scholarships to skateboarders who are high school seniors with a GPA of 2.5 or higher on a 4.0 scale. Recipients must enroll as a full-time undergraduate at an accredited college or university the fall after high school graduation. U.S. citizenship is required. The award is given to skateboard activists. The deadline is in late April. For more information visit www.skateboardscholarship.org.

6. Scholar Athlete Milk Mustache of the Year (SAMMY) Award

The Scholar Athlete Milk Mustache of the Year (SAMMY) Award is open to graduating high school senior scholar athletes. Candidates must demonstrate excellence in academics, athletic performance, leadership and community service. Candidates must also be a resident of one of the 48 contiguous states or the District of Columbia. There will be one scholarship of $7,500 awarded to each of 25 regional winners. The deadline is in early March. The www.whymilk. com web site includes photographs of previous winners with their milk mustaches. More information can be found at www.bodybymilk.com/sammy_scholarship.php.

7. National Marbles Tournament Scholarships

The annual National Marbles Tournament awards $5,000 in scholarships to mibsters (marble shooters) aged 8 to 14. The tournament is held in June each year. The children crowned King and Queen of Marbles each receive a $2,000 scholarship. A $1,000 scholarship is awarded to the boy and girl who win the sportsmanship award. For more information, visit www. nationalmarblestournament.org.

8. Klingon Language Institute Scholarship

   The Kor Memorial Scholarship is awarded by the Klingon Language Institute to recognize and encourage scholarship in the field of language study. Familiarity with Klingon or other constructed languages is not required, but creativity is preferred. The $500 award is open to undergraduate and graduate students. Nominations must be submitted by academic department chairs and/or deans. Only one undergraduate student and one graduate student may be nominated by each department chair or dean. The deadline is June 1. For more information, visit www.kli.org/scholarship.

9. National Beef Ambassador Program

   The National Beef Ambassador Program is a national public speaking competition for students aged 16 to 19. Winners are selected to represent the beef industry and win college scholarships and cash prizes. The cash prizes include $2,500 (1st place), $1,200 (2nd place) and $800 (3rd place). The scholarships, which are sponsored by the American National Cattlewomen Foundation, include $1,000 (1st place), $750 (2nd place) and $500 (3rd place). For more information, visit www.nationalbeefambassador.org.

10. Vegetarian Resource Group Scholarship

   The Vegetarian Resource Group (VRG) offers two $5,000 scholarships each year to graduating U.S. high school seniors who have promoted vegetarianism in their schools and communities. The application requires an essay about how the applicant promoted vegetarianism in their high school or community. The deadline is in February. Applications are available at www.vrg.org/student/scholar.htm.

For more information about these and dozens of other unusual scholarships, visit www.finaid.org/unusualscholarships.

Top Ten Most Prestigious Scholarships

Some of the most prestigious scholarships are also among the most generous scholarships. The prestigious scholarships that are also among the most generous scholarships are listed separately in the list of the top ten most generous undergraduate scholarships or the list of the top ten most generous graduate fellowships, which follow the list of the top ten most prestigious scholarships. Many prestigious scholarships require nomination by the student's school and involve study abroad after college graduation. They are also often extremely competitive.

1. Marshall Scholarships

    The Marshall Sherfield Scholarships Program is a highly competitive program in which up to 40 young Americans are chosen to pursue a graduate education in the United Kingdom each year. The awards are tenable at any British university and cover two years of study in any field, typically at the graduate level, leading to the award of a British university degree. The award provides for two years of study and may occasionally be extended to a third year. Only U.S. citizens who will have graduated with a Bachelor's degree from a four-year college or university in the United States within the past four years are eligible. A minimum 3.7 GPA (A-) on a 4.0 scale is required. Visit www.marshallscholarship.org for more information.

2. Rhodes Scholarship

    The Rhodes Scholarships enable students from many countries to study at the University of Oxford. 32 American Rhodes Scholars are selected each year. All educational expenses (tuition and fees) are covered for a period of two years, along with a maintenance allowance. Travel to and from Oxford is included. The award may be renewed for a third year. Visit www.rhodesscholar.org for more information.

3. Winston Churchill Scholarship Program

The Churchill Scholarship Program enables young Americans to pursue graduate study in science, mathematics and engineering at Churchill College, Cambridge University. A total of 11 one-year Churchill Scholarships are offered each year. The scholarship covers living expenses in addition to tuition and fees. Candidates must be U.S. citizens who have earned a Bachelor's degree but not a doctorate and between the ages of 19 and 26. Applicants must be nominated by their undergraduate college. Each college may nominate up to two students to apply for the Churchill Scholarship. The Churchill Foundation's deadline is in mid November. Each college may have earlier deadlines. For more information, visit www.winstonchurchillfoundation.org.

4. Harry S. Truman Scholarships

The Harry S. Truman Scholarships are open to college juniors who are U.S. citizens and nationals and who want to go to graduate school in preparation for a career in public service (government or the nonprofit and advocacy sectors). Truman Scholars are selected on the basis of their potential as future "change agents" who will improve the ways public entities serve the public good. Candidates should also have an extensive record of campus and community service. Candidates must be nominated by their college or university. Each college may nominate up to four students. (Four-year colleges and universities may also nominate up to three transfer students from two-year colleges.) Approximately 600 students are nominated and between 75 and 80 Truman Scholars are selected each year. The deadline is in early February. Visit www.truman.gov for more information.

5. Henry Luce Foundation Scholarship

The Luce Scholarships provide stipends and internships for 15-18 young Americans to live and work in Asia each year. Candidates must be U.S. citizens who have earned a

Bachelor's degree and are less than 30 years old as of July 1 the year they enter the program. The Luce Scholarship provides a monthly cost-of-living stipend plus travel expenses. Candidates are nominated by one of 75 colleges and universities. The foundation's deadline is December 1. Each college has an earlier deadline, typically in October. For more information, visit www.hluce.org/lsprogram.aspx.

6. Morris K. Udall Foundation Undergraduate Scholarships

The Morris K. Udall Foundation awards 80 undergraduate scholarships of up to $5,000 to college juniors and seniors in fields related to the environment, tribal public policy or Native American health care. An additional 30 students are named Honorable Mentions and receive awards of $350. Candidates must be nominated by their college's Udall faculty representative during their sophomore or junior year in college. Visit www.udall.gov for more information.

7. Robert C. Byrd Honors Scholarship Program

The Robert C. Byrd Honors Scholarship program is funded by the federal government and administered by the state governments in each state. This merit-based scholarship program is open to high school seniors who are U.S. citizens or permanent residents. Home-schooled students are eligible. Winners receive a $1,500 scholarship. Approximately 7,400 new scholars will be awarded each year. Students apply through the State education agency in their state of legal residence. Each state has its own deadlines. Visit www2. ed.gov/programs/iduesbyrd/ for more information.

8. Barry M. Goldwater Scholarship

The Barry M. Goldwater Scholarship program was established in 1986 by the United States Congress to honor Senator Barry M. Goldwater. Up to 300 Goldwater Scholarships are awarded each year. The scholarships cover tuition, fees, books and room and board up to a maximum of

$7,500 per year. (The scholarship is renewable for students who receive it during their junior year of college.) Each four-year institution may nominate up to four students who are currently sophomores or juniors for the award. Second-year students who are currently enrolled in a two-year college but intend to transfer to a four-year college or university are also eligible. The students must intend to pursue careers in math, science or engineering. (Students who plan on studying medicine are only eligible if they intend to pursue a career in medical research.) Candidates must have a GPA of at least 3.0 on a 4.0 scale and be in the upper quartile of his or her class. Candidates must be U.S. citizens, permanent residents or U.S. nationals. (Resident aliens must include a letter stating their intent to obtain U.S. citizenship and a copy of their Alien Registration Card.) Institutions must submit their nominations by January 31. Visit www.act.org/goldwater for more information.

9. Elie Wiesel Prize in Ethics Essay Contest

The Elie Wiesel Prize in Ethics Essay Contest is open to full-time juniors and seniors at accredited four-year colleges and universities in the United States. There is a first prize of $5,000, a second prize of $2,500, a third prize of $1,500 and two honorable mentions of $500 each. The deadline is in early December. Entry forms are available on the web site. For more information, write to The Elie Wiesel Prize in Ethics, The Elie Wiesel Foundation for Humanity, 555 Madison Avenue, 20th Floor, New York, NY 10022, fax 1-212-490-6006, send email to epinfo@eliewieselfoundation.org or visit www.eliewieselfoundation.org/entercontest.aspx.

10. National Merit Scholarship Corporation (NMSC)

The National Merit Scholarship Corporation (NMSC) sponsors the National Merit Scholarships and National Achievement Scholarships programs, as well as the Special Scholarships. These are among the largest scholarship competitions in the United States, with more than 10,000 students receiving college scholarships totaling $47 million. High school students enter the competitions by taking the PSAT test, also referred to as the National Merit Scholarship Qualifying Test (NMSQT). The top 16,000 or so students with the highest selection index scores are named Semifinalists. Of these, approximately 15,000 are named Finalists. 8,400 of the Finalists are selected to receive a National Merit Scholarship. An additional 1,600 participants who were not Finalists are selected for Special Scholarships sponsored by corporations. The National Achievement Scholarship Program recognizes outstanding African American students, with 1,600 being named Semifinalists. 1,300 of the Semifinalists are named Finalists and 775 Finalists are selected to receive the Achievement Scholarship. Scholarship amounts in both programs range from $2,500 to renewable four-year full tuition scholarships. Visit www.nationalmerit. org for more information.

For more information about these and dozens of other prestigious scholarships, visit www.finaid.org/prestigious.

Top Ten Most Generous Scholarships (Undergraduate)

1. Intel Science Talent Search

    The Intel Science Talent Search, previously known as the Westinghouse Science Talent Search, is one of the most prestigious scientific research competitions for high school seniors in the United States. Winners are selected on the basis of their potential as future scientists and researchers. Each year 300 students are named semifinalists and receive a $1,000 award. 40 of the semifinalists are named finalists and are invited on an all-expense-paid trip to the Science Talent Institute in Washington, DC in March, where the winners are selected. The first place finalist receives a $100,000 four-year scholarship, the second place finalist a $75,000 scholarship and the third place finalist a $50,000 scholarship. Fourth through sixth place finalists receive

$25,000 scholarships and seventh through tenth place finalists receive $20,000 scholarships. The remaining 30 finalists receive $5,000 scholarships. All finalists also receive a high performance computer. The entry deadline varies, but is typically in early to mid November. For more information, write to Society for Science and the Public, 1719 N Street, NW, Washington, DC 20036-2888, call 1-202-785-2255, send email to sts@societyforscience.org or visit www.intel.com/education/sts or www.societyforscience.org/sts.

2. Siemens Competition in Math, Science and Technology

The Siemens Competition in Math, Science and Technology is one of the most prestigious scientific research competitions for high school students in the United States. Students submit research reports individually or in teams of two or three. Some of the projects are selected for further competition in six regional events. One individual and one team are selected as Regional Winners and are invited to participate in the National Competition. The top individual and team winners at the National Competition receive $100,000 scholarships. The sixth through second place National Finalists receive scholarships ranging from $10,000 to $50,000. The Siemens Westinghouse Competition is administered by the College Board and funded by the Siemens Foundation. For more information write to Siemens Foundation, 170 Wood Avenue South, Iselin, NJ 08830, call 1-877-822-5233, fax 1-723-603-5890 or visit www.siemens-foundation.org/en/competition.htm.

3. NIH Undergraduate Scholarship Program

The NIH Undergraduate Scholarship Program (UGSP) is a competitive scholarship program sponsored by the National Institutes of Health (NIH) for students from disadvantaged backgrounds who are interested in pursuing biomedical, behavioral and social science careers at the NIH. The UGSP program provides up to $20,000 a year for up to four years to pay for tuition, educational expenses and reasonable living expenses. Approximately 15 scholarships are awarded each year. Recipients must participate in the NIH 10-week Summer Laboratory Experience after each year of scholarship support. Recipients also commit to one year of full-time employment at the NIH for each year of support. Candidates must have a GPA of 3.5 or higher on a 4.0 scale or be within the top 5 percent of their class. The deadline is February 28. Visit ugsp.nih.gov for more information.

4. Elks National Foundation Most Valuable Student Competition

The Elks National Foundation "Most Valuable Student" Competition awards 500 four-year scholarships to high school seniors. U.S. citizenship is required. (Resident alien status does not qualify.) Two renewable $15,000 scholarships, two renewable $10,000 scholarships, two renewable $5,000 scholarships, two renewable $4,000 scholarships, two renewable $3,000 scholarships, four renewable $2,500 scholarships, four renewable $2,000 scholarships and 482 renewable $1,000 scholarships are awarded each year for full-time enrollment in a four-year degree program at a U.S. college or university. Recipients are selected on the basis of scholarship, leadership and financial need. The application deadline is December 1. Contact your local Elks lodge, send email to scholarship@elks.org or visit www.elks.org/enf/scholars/mvs.cfm for more information. Applicants do not need to be related to a member of the Elks.

5. Davidson Fellows

Davidson Fellowships are awarded by the Davidson Institute for Talent Development to U.S. students under age 18 as of October 1 who have completed a significant piece of work in the fields of Mathematics, Science, Technology, Music, Literature, Philosophy or Outside the Box. The significant piece of work should have the potential to benefit society.

The focus of the program is on gifted and talented students. There is no minimum age for eligibility. Four $50,000 scholarships, seven $25,000 scholarships and five $10,000 scholarships are awarded each year. For more information, write to The Davidson Institute for Talent Development, Attn: Davidson Fellows Coordinators, 9665 Gateway Drive, Suite B, Reno, NV 89521, send email to DavidsonFellows@ davidsongifted.org or visit www.davidsonfellows.org.

6. Intel International Science and Engineering Fair

The Intel International Science and Engineering Fair (ISEF) is the world's largest science fair. Each year more than 1,500 students in grades 9-12 from more than 40 countries are selected at regional science fairs to compete at the ISEF for more than $4 million in scholarships and prizes. The top best in category winner receives a $75,000 scholarship. Two finalists receive the Intel Foundation Young Scientist scholarship of $50,000. The top three seniors receive a trip to the Nobel Prize ceremonies in Sweden. Other prizes include scholarships, summer internships, scientific field trips and laboratory equipment. A total of more than 900 individual and team awards are presented at the fair. For more information, write to Society for Science and the Public, 1719 N Street, NW, Washington, DC 20036-2888, call 1-202-785-2255 or visit www.intel.com/education/isef.

7. Rotary Foundation Ambassadorial Scholarships

The Rotary Foundation's Ambassadorial Scholarship program provides approximately 1,000 to 1,100 scholarships for study abroad each year. The scholarships are available for undergraduate and graduate students worldwide. (Applicants must be citizens of a country in which there is a Rotary club.) The scholarships cover one year of academic study in another country and include round-trip transportation, tuition, fees and room and board up to $25,000. Candidates must have completed at least two years of college. Applications are made through the local Rotary club. Each Rotary club has its own deadlines. Visit www. rotary.org for more information.

8. Collegiate Inventors Competition

    Sponsored by the National Inventors Hall of Fame, The Collegiate Inventors Competition (previously known as the BFGoodrich Collegiate Inventors Program) seeks to encourage undergraduate and graduate students to pursue new ideas, processes and technological innovations. The invention must have been reduced to practice and patentable. It may not have been made available to the public as a commercial product or process or been patented or published more than one year prior to the date of submission to the competition. Submissions are judged on originality and inventiveness, as well as on their potential value to society (socially, environmentally and economically) and on the range or scope of use. Up to four students may work together as a team, but only one prize will be awarded per entry. Graduate Collegiate Inventors Competition prizes include $15,000 (Gold), $10,000 (Silver) and $5,000 (Bronze). Undergraduate Collegiate Inventors Competition prizes include $10,000 (Gold), $5,000 (Silver) and $2,500 (Bronze). The deadline is June 1. For more information, write to The Collegiate Inventors Competition, c/o Invent Now, 3701 Highland Park NW, North Canton, OH 44720-4535 or visit www.invent.org/collegiate.

9. Coca-Cola Scholars Program Scholarship

    The Coca-Cola Scholars Foundation Scholarships are open to U.S. high school seniors who have a GPA of at least 3.0 on a 4.0 scale. A total of 250 scholarships are awarded each year, with 50 National Scholars receiving $20,000 scholarships and 200 Regional Scholars receiving $10,000 scholarships. (The Coca-Cola Scholars Foundation also awards 50 $2,000 scholarships and 350 $1,000 scholarships to outstanding community college students.) Recipients are selected based on leadership, character, civic and extracurricular activities, academic excellence and community service. This is an extremely competitive program, with more than 100,000 applications received each year. The application deadline is in late October or early November. For more information, call 1-800-306-COKE (1-800-306-2653), send email to scholars@ na.ko.com or visit www.coca-colascholars.org.

10. Gates Millennium Scholars

The Gates Millennium Scholars program is sponsored by the Bill and Melinda Gates Foundation and administered by the United Negro College Fund. Nomination by a professional educator (principal, teacher, guidance counselor, etc.) is required. The focus of this program is on students who will be pursuing careers in mathematics, science, engineering, education or library science. Candidates must be African America, American Indian/Alaskan Native, Asian Pacific Islander American or Hispanic American, a U.S. citizen or permanent resident/national, have a cumulative GPA of 3.3 on a 4.0 scale and be entering a U.S. accredited college or university as a full-time degree-seeking freshman in the fall. Candidates must also be eligible for the Federal Pell Grant. Nominations must be submitted by early to mid January. Applications must be submitted by February 1. For more information, write to Gates Millennium Scholars, PO Box 10500, Fairfax, VA 22031-8044, call 1-877-690-GMSP (1-877-690-4677) or visit www.gmsp.org.

Also noteworthy is the Jack Kent Cooke Foundation (JKCF). Their Young Scholars Program is one of the most personalized and generous scholarship programs in the U.S. About 50 7th grade students are selected each year and receive undergraduate and graduate support from the foundation. The Undergraduate Transfer Scholarship provides up to $30,000 per year for about 50 community college students to help them transfer to four-year colleges and universities to obtain a Bachelor's degree. For more information, call 1-800-498-6478 or visit www.jackkentcookefoundation.org.

Top Ten Most Generous Fellowships (Graduate)

1. National Science Foundation Graduate Research Fellowship

   The U.S. National Science Foundation (NSF) Graduate Research Fellowship awards approximately 900 to 1,000 new three-year fellowships each year to graduate students in the mathematical, physical, biological, engineering and behavioral and social sciences. (The full list of eligible fields is: animal sciences, anthropology, archeology, astronomy, biochemistry, bioengineering, biophysics & structural biology, chemical engineering, chemistry, civil & environmental engineering, computer science, cultural anthropology, ecology, economics, electrical engineering, engineering fields, environmental life sciences, genetics & evolutionary biology, geography, geosciences, history of science, linguistics, materials engineering, mathematical sciences, mechanical engineering, microbiology & cell biology, molecular & developmental biology, neurosciences & physiology, physics, plant & other life sciences, political science, psychology, public policy, sociology.) The award consists of a $10,500 cost-of-education allowance in lieu of tuition and fees and a $30,000 annual living stipend, as well as access to supercomputing facilities. College seniors and first year graduate students are eligible to apply. Candidates must be U.S. citizens, nationals or permanent residents. The application deadline is in early November. Visit www.nsfgradfellows.org for more information.

2. National Defense Science and Engineering Graduate Fellowships (NDSEG)

   The National Defense Science and Engineering Graduate Fellowships are sponsored by the U.S. Department of Defense and support graduate students pursuing a doctoral degree in Aeronautical and Astronautical Engineering, Biosciences, Chemical Engineering, Chemistry, Civil Engineering, Cognitive, Neural and Behavioral Sciences Computer and Computational Sciences, Electrical Engineering, Geosciences, Materials Science and Engineering, Mathematics, Mechanical Engineering, Naval Architecture and Ocean Engineering, Oceanography and Physics. Approximately 100 to 300 new fellowships are awarded each year, depending on funding. Candidates must be U.S. citizens or nationals. College seniors and first-year graduate students are eligible to apply. The fellowship provides full tuition and required fees and an annual stipend for three years. The application deadline is in early January. The fellowship program is very competitive, with only about 10% of applicants being selected for the award. For more information, write to NDSEG Fellowship Program, American Society for Engineering Education, 1818 N Street N.W., Suite 600, Washington, DC 20036, call 1-202-331-3546, fax 1-202-265-8504, send email to ndseg@asee.org or visit ndseg.asee.org.

3. Hertz Foundation Graduate Fellowships in Applied Physical Sciences

    The Hertz Foundation Graduate Fellowships are awarded to graduate students who are expected to have the greatest impact on the application of the physical sciences to human problems. The Hertz Foundation Graduate Fellowships are extremely competitive, with only 25% of applicants being selected for an interview and only 10% of those being selected for the award. The fellowship consists of a cost-of-education allowance and a $31,000 stipend and is renewable for a total of up to five years of support. College seniors and current graduate students pursuing a PhD in the applied physical sciences are eligible to apply. The fellowship is tenable at fifty of the nation's leading colleges and universities, including California Institute of Technology, Carnegie Mellon University, Harvard University, Johns Hopkins University,

Massachusetts Institute of Technology (MIT), Princeton, RPI, Rice, Stanford, UC Berkeley and Yale, among others. For more information, visit www.hertzfoundation.org.

4. NASA Graduate Student Researchers Program (GSRP)

The NASA Graduate Student Researchers Program (GSRP) provides fellowships for graduate study leading to a Master's or doctoral degree in science, mathematics and engineering. Approximately 150 new recipients are selected each year. The award consists of a one-year training grant of $27,000, renewable for up to three years. The training grant includes a stipend of $20,000, a student allowance of $6,000, a student health insurance allowance of $1,000 and a university allowance of $3,000. U.S. citizenship is required. College seniors and current graduate students are eligible to apply. The application deadline is in early March. Visit fellowships.hq.nasa.gov/gsrp for more information.

5. Jacob K. Javits Graduate Fellowships

The Jacob K. Javits Graduate Fellowships are awarded by the U.S. Department of Education to support graduate students in the arts, humanities and social sciences. The fellowship consists of a payment to the educational institution in lieu of tuition and fees and a stipend of up to $30,000 for up to four years. The amount of funding depends on financial need and applications are required to submit the Free Application for Federal Student Aid. The program is open to undergraduate students who are about to enter graduate school and first year graduate students. Candidates must be enrolled or intend to enroll in a graduate program leading to a doctorate or terminal Master's degree. Candidates must be U.S. citizens, nationals or permanent residents. The application deadline is September 30. A total of approximately 60 to 100 new fellowships are awarded each year. This is an extremely competitive program. Visit www2.ed.gov/programs/jacobjavits for more information.

6. National Physical Science Consortium Fellowship

    The National Physical Science Consortium (NPSC) sponsors a graduate fellowship program for graduate students pursuing a PhD in the physical sciences at one of more than 100 participating colleges and universities. The award provides tuition and fees and a stipend of $20,000 for up to six years. Recipients are required to work for a NPSC-member employer during the summer preceding and following the first year of graduate school. Fields of study include Astronomy, Chemistry, Computer Science, Geology, Materials Science, Mathematical Sciences, Physics and their sub-disciplines and related engineering fields, including Chemical, Computer, Electrical, Environmental and Mechanical Engineering. NPSC continues to place an emphasis on recruiting underrepresented minority and female students. U.S. citizenship is required. College seniors and first year graduate students are eligible to apply. A minimum GPA of 3.0 on a 4.0 scale is required. The application deadline is November 30. Visit www.npsc.org for more information.

7. Beinecke Scholarship Program

    The Beinecke Scholarship Program is open to college juniors who intend to pursue graduate study in the arts, humanities and social sciences at any accredited university. Each scholar receives $4,000 prior to matriculating in graduate school and $30,000 while attending graduate school. The funding must be used within five years of completing undergraduate studies. A total of 18 new scholarships are awarded each year from among more than 100 nominations. Nomination by a participating college or university is required. The nomination deadline is late February or early March and each college can nominate only one student for the award. For more information, visit www.beineckescholarship.org.

8. Wenner-Gren Fellowships

    The Wenner-Gren Foundation awards grants of up to $25,000 for Dissertation Fieldwork for basic research in anthropology. (They also award $25,000 Post-PhD Grants and $40,000 Richard Carely Hunt Postdoctoral Fellowships for research in anthropology.) Candidates for the Dissertation Fieldwork Grants must be enrolled in a program leading to a doctoral degree and must complete all requirements for the degree other than the dissertation. Applications are made jointly with the candidate's thesis advisor or other scholar who will supervise the project. U.S. citizenship is not required. Deadlines are May 1 and January 1. For more information, call 1-212-683-5000, fax 1-212-683-9151, write to The Wenner-Gren Foundation, 470 Park Avenue South, 8th Floor, New York, NY 10016-6819, send email to inquiries@ wennergren.org or visit www.wennergren.org/programs.

9. Social Science Research Council – International Dissertation Research Fellowship

    The Social Science Research Council and the American Council of Learned Societies sponsor the International Dissertation Field Research Fellowship (IDRF) program for graduate students in humanities and social sciences conducting doctoral dissertation field research outside the United States. A total of 50 fellowships of approximately $20,000 each are awarded each year with funds provided by the Andrew W. Mellon Foundation. The fellowships provide support for nine to twelve months of dissertation research. Candidates must be full-time graduate students attending doctoral programs in the U.S., but do not need to be U.S. citizens. There is an emphasis on research that is engaged in interdisciplinary and cross-regional perspectives. Recipients must have completed all PhD requirements except for fieldwork and the on-site dissertation research by the start of their fellowship or December of the award year, whichever comes first. The application deadline is in early November.

For more information, visit www.ssrc.org/programs/idrf or send email to idrf@ssrc.org.

10. Gates Cambridge Scholarships

The Gates Cambridge Scholarships are open to graduate students from outside the United Kingdom for study at the University of Cambridge. Approximately 230 scholarships are awarded each year, with 100 coming from the United States. The scholarships cover the full cost of study at Cambridge for a single person, including tuition and fees and a maintenance allowance. Scholars should be under the age of 30 years and be admitted through the university's regular admissions process. Visit www.gates.scholarships. cam.ac.uk for more information.

Also noteworthy are the Fulbright Fellowships, which provide funding for U.S. citizens to study in other countries and for international students to study in the U.S. U.S. students must apply through their campus Fulbright program advisor. International students should apply through the Fulbright Commission or U.S. Information Service in their home country. Visit www.iie.org/ fulbright for more information.

Top Ten Scholarships for Children Age 13 and Under

You don't have to be a high school senior to apply for scholarships. There are many scholarships available to current college students as well as high school freshmen, sophomores and juniors. There are even many scholarships for students in grades K-8 or who are age 13 and under.

1. National Spelling Bee

The National Spelling Bee is sponsored by the E.W. Scripps Company. It is open to students in grades 1-8 as of their school finals (February 1) and who are under age 16 as of the date of the national finals (June 1). The champion wins a total of $28,000 in cash prizes and scholarships. The second place finisher wins a cash prize of $6,000, the third place finisher receives $3,500, the fourth place finisher receives $2,000, the fifth place finisher receives $1,250, the sixth place finisher receives $1,000 and the seventh place finisher receives $750. There are also assorted other prizes ranging from $50 to $600 for students who are eliminated in earlier rounds. (There is a $99 school registration fee.) For more information, visit www.spellingbee.com.

2. National Geography Bee

    The National Geography Bee is sponsored by the National Geographic Society. It is open to U.S. students in grades 4-8 who are age 15 or younger by the date of the national competition. The National Geography Bee is a three stage competition, starting at the school level (competitions from mid-November through mid-January), followed by state competitions in April and the national competition in May. The ten finalists compete for college scholarships. The first place winner receives a $25,000 scholarship, the second place winner a $15,000 scholarship and the third place winner a $10,000 scholarship. The school registration deadline is October 15. (There is a $90 school registration fee.) For more information, call 1-202-828-6659 or write to National Geographic Bee, National Geographic Society, 1145 17th Street N.W., Washington, DC 20036-4688 or visit www.nationalgeographic.com/geobee/.

3. National History Day Contest

    The National History Day Contest is open to students in grades 6-12 in the junior (grades 6-8) and senior (grades 9-12) divisions. The projects relate to a specific historical topic or theme. There are seven categories, including individual papers, individual exhibits, group exhibits, individual performance, group performance, individual documentary and group documentation. Within each category, the first place winner receives $1,000, the second place winner receives

$500 and the third place winner receives $250. The national contest is held in June. Visit www.nationalhistoryday.org/Contest.htm for more information.

4. Jif Most Creative Peanut Butter Sandwich Contest

Jif Most Creative Peanut Butter Sandwich Contest is open to children who are age 6 to 12. The grand prize is a $25,000 scholarship fund. The four runners up receive a $2,500 scholarship fund. The deadline is mid-November. The contest is sponsored by the J.M. Smucker Company. Visit promotions.jif.com/most-creative-contest for more information.

5. Scholastic Art & Writing Awards

The Scholastic Art & Writing Awards are open to U.S. and Canadian students in grades 7-12. It is sponsored by Scholastic Inc. and administered by the Alliance for Young Artists and Writers, Inc. More than 250,000 students enter the competition each year. Gold Portfolio Award recipients receive $10,000 scholarships (8 visual artists and 7 writers). For more information, send email to info@artandwriting.org or visit www.artandwriting.org.

6. Christopher Columbus Community Service Awards

The Christopher Columbus Community Service Awards are open to teams of students in grades 6-8. The competition focuses on using science and technology to solve real-world community problems. Each member of the winning teams receives a $2,000 U.S. Savings Bond. Winners also receive a trip to the National Championship Week at Walt Disney World. One team will receive the $25,000 Columbus Foundation Community Grant to fund the implementation of their idea. The competition is sponsored by the Christopher Columbus Fellowship Foundation in cooperation with the National Science Foundation. The deadline is the second Monday in February. For more information, call 1-800-291-

6020, fax 1-215-579-8589, write to Christopher Columbus Awards, 105 Terry Drive, Suite 120, Newtown, PA 18940-3425, send email to success@edumedia.com or visit www. christophercolumbusawards.com.

7. Dick Blick Linoleum Block Print Contest

Dick Blick sponsors an annual contest for block prints made from linoleum. There are three divisions: grades 4-6, grades 7-9 and grades 10-12. Within each division there is one first prize of $400, one second prize of $250, one third prize of $150 and two honorable mentions of $50. The prizes are in the form of art materials chosen by the winner's teacher from Dick Blick's catalog for use in the winner's art class. The deadline is March 15. For more information, call 1-800-828-4548, fax 1-800-621-8293, write to Artsonia, ATTN: Linoleum Contest, 3166 North Lincoln Avenue, Suite 416, Chicago, IL 60657, send email to info@dickblick.com or visit www.dickblick.com/blockcontest.

8. Gloria Barron Prize for Young Heroes

The Gloria Barron Prize for Young Heroes is awarded annually to ten U.S. and Canadian students, aged 8-18, who have developed an extraordinary service project that helped people and the planet. Half of the winners are focused on helping their communities and people and half are focused on protecting the environment. Winners receive a $2,500 scholarship. For more information, write to The Barron Prize, 545 Pearl Street, Boulder, CO 80302 or visit www. barronprize.org.

9. Patriot's Pen

Patriot's Pen is an essay writing contest (patriotic theme) sponsored by the Veterans of Foreign Wars (VFW). It is open to U.S. students in grades 6-8. More than 115,000 students enter the contest each year. The first place winner receives a $10,000 U.S. Savings Bond. The 28 top national winners receive U.S. Savings Bonds of $1,000 to $10,000. Entries are submitted through local VFW Posts. The contest is also known as the VFW Youth Essay Contest. The deadline is November 1. For more information, call 1-816-968-1117 or visit www.vfw.org.

10. Prudential Spirit of Community Awards

The Prudential Spirit of Community Awards recognize children in grades 5-12 who have engaged in volunteer activities and have demonstrated exceptional community service. The program is sponsored by Prudential in conjunction with the National Association of Secondary School Principals (NASSP). State winners receive a $1,000 award. National winners receive a $5,000 award. The student application deadline is November 1. For more information, visit www.prudential.com/community/spirit/awards.

For more information about these and other scholarships for younger students, visit www.finaid.org/age13.

Top Ten Scholarships for Community Service

What better way to earn money for college than to help your community? These scholarships reward and recognize outstanding community service by students and young adults.

1. Segal AmeriCorps Education Award

The Segal AmeriCorps Education Award provides several thousand dollars for each year of full-time service (prorated for part-time). Through 2009 the maximum education award was $4,725. Starting in 2010 the maximum education award is pegged to the maximum Pell Grant. The money can be used to pay for college costs or to repay student loans. The award may be claimed up to seven years after the service is completed. Visit www.americorps.gov for more information.

2. The Do Something Awards

The Do Something Awards provide community grants and scholarships to "change-makers" age 25 and under who work with Do Something to improve their communities. The competition is open to U.S. and Canadian citizens and permanent residents. Five Do Something Award nominees will receive at least $10,000 in community grants and scholarships. Of the five winners, one grand prize winner will receive a total of $100,000 in community grants. The nominees also participate in a live VH1 TV show and will receive continued support from DoSomething.org. (The community grants are paid to the nominee's organization or a not-for-profit organization of the nominee's choice. All winners have the option of receiving $5,000 of the total award in the form of a college scholarship.) The deadline is March 1. For more information, send email to dsawards@dosomething.org or visit www.dosomething.org/programs/awards.

3. Comcast Leaders and Achievers Scholarship Program

The Comcast Leaders and Achievers Scholarship Program, formerly the Comcast Foundation Leaders of Tomorrow Scholarship Program, awards more than one thousand $1,000 scholarships for community service and leadership to high school seniors in communities served by Comcast. Candidates must be nominated by their high school principals by mid-March. Each principal may nominate only one student. Visit www.comcast.com/Corporate/About/InTheCommunity/Partners/LeadersAndAchievers.html for more information.

4. Discover Card Tribute Award

The Discover Card Tribute Award awards up to $1 million in scholarships annually to high school juniors nationwide. Discover awards up to 300 state scholarships of $2,500 and up to ten national $25,000 scholarships. The scholarships may be used for postsecondary education at two and four-year colleges and trade/technical schools. Winners are selected on the basis of community service, special talents, leadership and overcoming an obstacle. Candidates must have a GPA of 2.75 or better in the 9th and 10th grades. The deadline is in late January or early February. For more information, call 1-866-756-7932 or visit www.discoverfinancial.com/community.

5. Echoing Green Fellowship

The Echoing Green Fellowship provides 12-20 two-year $60,000 grant ($30,000 per year) to individuals age 18 or older to develop and implement a community service project. (Note that this is not a scholarship per se, but seed money to establish a community service organization.) The project must be in the start-up phase. Lobbying activities, research projects and faith-based initiatives are not eligible. The deadline is in early November. For more information, call 1-212-689-1165, fax 1-212-689-9010, write to Echoing Green, 494 Eighth Avenue, 2nd Floor, New York, NY 10001, send email to info@echoinggreen.org or visit www.echoinggreen.org.

6. The Heart of America Christopher Reeve Award

The Heart of America Christopher Reeve Award is awarded annually to a student for extraordinary community service. The award includes a $1,000 scholarship. Candidates must be a senior in high school or younger when awarded. The deadline is October 31. Visit www.heartofamerica.org/scholarships.htm for more information.

7. Kohl's Kids Who Care Program

The Kohl's Kids Who Care Program (www.kohlskids.com) honors students age 6-18 who are involved in community service. Candidates enter by being nominated by an adult age 21 years or older. Nominees are considered in two age groups, 6-12 and 13-18, with three prize levels within each group. More than 2,100 children will receive a total of more than $410,000 in scholarships and prizes. More than 2,100 store winners each receive a $50 Kohl's gift card, 200 regional winners each receive a $1,000 scholarship and 10 national winners each receive a $10,000 scholarship. The deadline is March 15. Visit www.kohlscorporation. com/CommunityRelations/scholarship/index.asp for more information.

8. Samuel Huntington Public Service Award

The Samuel Huntington Public Service Award provides a $10,000 stipend to a graduating college senior to pursue a year of public service anywhere in the world. The money may be used for any project that helps others. Candidates submit a proposal as part of their application. U.S. citizenship is not required. The deadline is in mid-January. For more information, visit www.nationalgridus.com/masselectric/about_us/award.asp.

9. National Caring Award

The National Caring Award is sponsored by the Caring Institute and the Pay It Forward Foundation. Each year 10 adults and 5 young adults (12th grade and below) are recognized through this program. The young adults each receive a $2,000 scholarship. Visit www.caringinstitute.org for more information.

10. Youth Action Net

Youth Action Net awards twenty small grants to youth leaders aged 18-29 for projects that promote social change in their communities. The deadline is October 1. Visit www. youthactionnet.org for more information.

For more information about these and dozens of other scholarships for volunteering and community service, visit www.finaid.org/volunteering.

Top Ten Scholarships That Don't Require an A

Ordinary students often ask whether there are any scholarships available to students who don't have an A average. Although these scholarships don't require a high GPA, they do require excellence in a non-academic area. Every scholarship sponsor is trying to find the students that best fulfill their selection criteria. If a scholarship program's selection criteria don't depend on academic merit, then they might depend on athletic or artistic merit, community service, extracurricular activities or on skill in a non-academic discipline. The winners are always the students who best reflect the goals of the scholarship sponsor. Candidates don't necessarily need to be academically talented, but do need to be extraordinary and amazing in other ways.

In addition to the following scholarship programs, many of the scholarships listed in some of the other top ten lists do not depend on grades. These include the lists of community service scholarships and unusual scholarships. For example, the David Letterman Telecommunications Scholarship and the Duck Brand Duct Tape Stuck at Prom Contest require applicants to demonstrate non-academic creativity.

1. U.S. Department of Education

    Federal education grants, like the Pell Grant, are based on financial need. Most recipients of the Pell Grant have family income under $50,000. But the need analysis formula is complicated and depends not just on income and assets, but also on the number of children enrolled in college at the same time. A very small percentage of Pell Grant recipients have income over $100,000. However, even wealthy families can qualify for federal education loans, such as the unsubsidized Stafford loan and the Parent PLUS loan. Recipients of federal student aid must maintain at least a C cumulative grade point average. Visit www.fafsa.ed.gov to apply.

    The federal government also provides a variety of education tax benefits, such as the Hope Scholarship tax credit, that do not dependent on grades. Visit www.finaid.org/taxbenefits for more information.

2. AXA Achievement Scholarship Program

    The AXA Achievement Scholarship Program awards more than $1.3 million a year to high school seniors who have demonstrated outstanding achievement in non-academic activities in school, community or workplace. The award is sponsored by the AXA Foundation. U.S. citizenship or legal residency is required. The program includes scholarships of $25,000, $10,000 and $2,000. Visit www.axa-achievement. com for more information and application forms.

3. Horatio Alger Association Scholarships

    The Horatio Alger Association provides scholarships for students who have demonstrated integrity and perseverance in overcoming adversity. Other selection criteria include strength of character, financial need, a good academic record (a GPA of 2.0 or higher) and a desire to contribute to society. The association awards more than 100 $20,000 national scholarships and many state scholarships each year to high school seniors. U.S. citizenship is required. Several state affiliates also have state scholarship programs. The deadline is October 15. Visit www.horatioalger.com/scholarships for more information.

4. Ayn Rand Institute

    The Ayn Rand Institute sponsors several essay contests based on books written by Ayn Rand.

    The *Anthem Essay Contest* is open to high school freshmen and sophomores. It provides annual cash awards for short, original, unpublished essays on the philosophic themes in Ayn Rand's novel, *Anthem*. The first prize is $2,000. There are five second prizes of $500 and ten third prizes of $200. The deadline is in mid-March.

The *Fountainhead Essay Contest* is open to high school juniors and seniors. It provides annual cash awards for short, original, unpublished essays on the philosophic themes in Ayn Rand's novel, *The Fountainhead*. The first prize is $10,000. There are five second place prizes of $2,000 and ten third place prizes of $1,000. The deadline is in mid-April.

The *We the Living Essay Contest* is open to high school sophomores, juniors and seniors. It provides annual cash awards for short, original, unpublished essays on the philosophic themes in Ayn Rand's novel, *We the Living*. The first prize is $3,000. There are five second place prizes of $1,000 and five third place prizes of $300. The deadline is in early May.

The *Atlas Shrugged Essay Contest* is open to high school seniors and all undergraduate and graduate students. It provides annual cash awards for short, original, unpublished essays on the philosophic themes in Ayn Rand's novel, *Atlas Shrugged*. The first prize is $10,000. There are three second prizes of $2,000 and five third prizes of $1,000. The deadline is in mid-September.

For more information, send email to essays@aynrand.org or visit www.aynrand.org/contests.

5. Girls Going Places Scholarship

The Girls Going Places Scholarship is sponsored by Guardian Life Insurance Company of America. It awards prizes totaling $30,000 to 15 girls aged 12-18 who have demonstrated budding entrepreneurship. There is one first place award of $10,000, one second place award of $5,000, one third place award of $3,000 and twelve $1,000 awards. The competition starts September 1. The deadline is March 1. Visit www.guardianlife.com/womens_channel/girls_going_places/girls_going_places.html for more information.

6. Holocaust Remembrance Project Essay Contest

The Holocaust Remembrance Project Essay Contest is designed to encourage and promote the study of the Holocaust. Ten first place winners receive an all-expense-paid trip to Washington DC to visit the U.S. Holocaust Memorial Museum and scholarships of $2,500 to $5,000. The contest is open to all residents of the United States and Mexico and also to U.S. Citizens living abroad. Candidates should be enrolled in high school (grades 9-12) and age 19 or younger. The deadline is April 15. For more information, send email to holocaust@hklaw.com or visit holocaust.hklaw.com.

7. Americanism Essay Contest

The Americanism Essay Contest is sponsored by the Fleet Reserve Association (FRA) National Committee on Americanism-Patriotism. Awards include a Grand National prize of a $10,000 U.S. Savings Bond and $5,000, $3,000 and $2,000 U.S. Savings Bonds awarded to the first, second and third place winners in each grade category. The contest is open to students in grades 7 through 12. Entrants must be sponsored by a FRA member or by a chartered branch or unit. The deadline is December 1. Visit www.fra.org/Content/fra/AboutFRA/EssayContest for more information.

8. AFSA National Scholarship Essay Contest

The AFSA National Scholarship Essay Contest is sponsored by the American Fire Sprinkler Association. There are ten $2,000 scholarships (high school seniors) and five $1,000 scholarships (high school graduates or GED recipients). Information is available starting in the fall. For more information, visit www.afsascholarship.org.

9. Red Vines Drawing Contest

Sponsored by the American Licorice Company, the Red Vines Drawing Contest is open to children in three age groups (as of May 1): kids (ages 6-12), teens (ages 13-18) and adult (ages 19+). In each age group and entry format there is one first prize winner of a $2,500 scholarship, one second prize of $250 and one third prize of $100. Entries (one per person) consist of an original work of art that features the Red Vines logo. Winners will be selected on the basis of creativity and relevance to the Red Vines brand candy. The deadline is September 30. For more information, visit www.redvines.com/drawingcontest.html or write to American Licorice Co., 2796 NW Clearwater Drive, Bend, OR 97701.

10. Community Foundation Scholarships

Many community foundations have several scholarship funds with either no academic requirements or which use the same cumulative GPA standard as for the Federal Pell Grant, namely a 2.0+ GPA. A list of community foundations can be found at www.foundations.org/communityfoundations.html. You can also use the Foundation Center's *Foundation Finder* tool at foundationcenter.org/findfunders/foundfinder/ to find your local community foundation.

NOTES

SCHOLARSHIP CHECKLIST

Scholarship Name	Deadline	Application Requirements
	Date Due: □ Postmark □ Receipt Date Mailed:	□ Application Form □ Essays □ Interview □ Recommendations (# __) □ Resume □ Official Academic Transcripts □ Test Scores (SAT/ACT) □ Tax Returns □ FAFSA (SAR) □ Proofread Application □ Keep a Copy of the Application
	Date Due: □ Postmark □ Receipt Date Mailed:	□ Application Form □ Essays □ Interview □ Recommendations (# __) □ Resume □ Official Academic Transcripts □ Test Scores (SAT/ACT) □ Tax Returns □ FAFSA (SAR) □ Proofread Application □ Keep a Copy of the Application
	Date Due: □ Postmark □ Receipt Date Mailed:	□ Application Form □ Essays □ Interview □ Recommendations (# __) □ Resume □ Official Academic Transcripts □ Test Scores (SAT/ACT) □ Tax Returns □ FAFSA (SAR) □ Proofread Application □ Keep a Copy of the Application
	Date Due: □ Postmark □ Receipt Date Mailed:	□ Application Form □ Essays □ Interview □ Recommendations (# __) □ Resume □ Official Academic Transcripts □ Test Scores (SAT/ACT) □ Tax Returns □ FAFSA (SAR) □ Proofread Application □ Keep a Copy of the Application

- Search for scholarships at free web sites like www.fastweb.com and www.finaid.org. Answer all of the optional questions to maximize your matches.

- Visit the local library or bookstore for scholarship books and guidance counselor and financial aid offices for local awards.

- Ask employers, unions, fraternal organizations, religious organizations, cultural and ethnic groups, volunteer groups, clubs, the PTA and local businesses about scholarships.

- Do not pay money to search for scholarships or to apply for a scholarship.

8158831R0

Made in the USA
Charleston, SC
13 May 2011